A
Piece
of
Me
Is
Missing

A Piece of Me Is Missing

MARILYN CRAM DONAHUE

TYNDALE HOUSE PUBLISHERS, INC.
Wheaton, Illinois

Library of Congress Catalog Card Number 78-58747
ISBN 0-8423-4828-X, paper
Copyright ©1978 by Marilyn Cram Donahue
Wheaton, Illinois. All rights reserved.

First printing, September 1978
Printed in the United States of America.

*To all of you who
in your commitment to life, are willing
to lift up your hearts and reach beyond the stars.*

ACKNOWLEDGMENTS

Grateful acknowledgment is given to the following publications for granting permission to reprint in this book the following previously published material: "How Does Your Garden Grow?" in *Today's Christian Parent,* copyright Autumn 1977, The Standard Publishing Company. "The Touch Me Not," in *Today's Christian Parent,* copyright Spring 1977, The Standard Publishing Company. "A Real High," in *Listen,* copyright October 1977, Narcotics Education, Inc. "God Shared His Laughter," in *The Lutheran,* copyright August 1977, the Lutheran Church in America. "Take a Coffee Break with God," in *Lutheran Standard,* copyright 1971, Augsburg Publishing House.

CONTENTS

INTRODUCTION

Literally hundreds of books and thousands of magazine articles have been written about self-improvement and problem-solving. We women are told how to improve our figures, dispositions, marriages, homes, and our children's grades at school. We are instructed in money management, housekeeping techniques, cookery, and interior decorating . . . all of which tell us nothing about our real problems. Our inside problems. The ones that deal with who we really are . . . and who we want to become.

Unfortunately, most of the literature that tries to crack the shells of our tough exteriors is clothed in idealism and gilded with technical language. Nobody tells us in a few simple words what the real problem is. Nobody gives us simple, practical ways to solve our dilemma. I'm talking about step-by-step instructions clothed in nothing but everyday language with some specific examples thrown in.

What we need is not an extended ego trip. What we need is help! The cry is universal: "Part of me is missing, and I don't know how to find it!" There's your problem. Listen to it in discontented voices. Hear it in petty jealousies. See it in eyes filled with uncertainty, fear, hate. Feel it in hands that tremble. Find it in loneliness, boredom, and despair.

This is not the way we were meant to be. We were created whole. Somewhere along the way, you and I lost little pieces of ourselves. It happens as easily as losing parts of a jigsaw puzzle. The pieces get pushed carelessly to the edge of the table until, unnoticed, they drop out of sight. If you don't look carefully, you may never see them again.

A piece of me is missing! Part of you is missing too! And that's the way it's going to be until we become the kind of people we were meant to be. I'm talking about a vision . . . the vision God has for the best that is in each

of us. If you want to give it a name, you can call it
abundant life. If you want proof, look it up for yourself.
It's in John 10:10: "I came that they may have life,
and have it abundantly." It's God's promise. It's a gift, if
you can only reach out and take it.

But how? How do you handle a vision? How do you, as
a woman, handle the challenge of God's great plan? How
do you reach out for perfection when the dinner is late,
and all you can hear are record players and hungry
youngsters? How can you find peace of mind and soul
and body when Johnny spills his milk, and it runs into
your lap? Or when the boss asks you to work overtime
when your family is counting on you for a homemade
birthday cake?

How can you . . . and you . . . and you . . . deal with
flat tires and burned toast and a souffle that just fell and
a dog that hates the mailman and still manage to keep
your head on straight and your heart full of love . . . let
alone deal with a vision?

You have to start somewhere. You started already
when you saw the title of this book and recognized
yourself in the words on the cover. But that wasn't
enough. If God's vision is a gift, it's also a goal, and you
don't reach goals, at least not entirely, by dreaming. You
have to take practical steps, or you're in trouble.

I once read a science fiction story about a race of
people who became so involved in mental exploration and
daydreaming that eventually they were unable to cope
with the ordinary problems of everyday living. They even
forgot how to operate the machines that they had
invented. They became totally helpless, ineffectual
beings. Science fiction? Not entirely!

Daydreaming, you see, is not the way to handle a
vision. That may be the way visions begin, but that's not
the way they're activated. We women, in particular, know
what happens to our homes when our hands are idle for
too long. Too much dreaming of a better world with a
better you in it . . . too much wishing you were somewhere
else . . . does not get the dust off the coffee table. Neither

does it get you off your hands and knees in the middle of a dirty kitchen floor.

Don't misunderstand. I'm not advocating a life of drudgery. I hope your vision goes *beyond* your floor. There was a time in my life when I limited my vision to the top of the broom handle. It was during those years when I had four preschool children . . . all home . . . all day. It seemed that all I did was clean up after somebody. It wasn't really so bad. After all, someone had to do it. But I made the same mistake I've noticed in lots of other women. I let my vision level drop. Cleaning became my occupation. I made a fetish of my clean house. I didn't neglect my family because of it, but I surely neglected myself! It was not abundant living.

Finally, one day, my husband said a shocking thing to me, and it changed my life. "You know what they're going to say about you when you're gone?" he asked.

At that point in time, I wasn't planning on "going," but I couldn't wait to hear what he was going to say, because I expected some sort of compliment for my war against dirt and germs.

He patted me on the back. "They're going to say," he told me, "that you kept a good floor."

That did it. If there was anything I wanted to be remembered for, the kitchen floor was definitely not it. This doesn't mean that I immediately reverted to keeping a dirty house. I just decided to get the work done quickly and go on to something better.

Your vision has to be a lot higher than the broom handle, but it should never be too high for you to reach toward. It's just that all of us need some sort of plan. That's what this book is all about. The following pages are filled with twelve months' worth of practical suggestions—ways you can reach out toward becoming the person God intended you to be . . . the ideal you . . . while you're busy with the business of everyday living.

Each chapter is assigned to a particular month of the year. You don't have to start reading in January. Whatever month it is when you open this book, that's where you start. Although all the chapters are closely related, leading step by step to a single goal, they also stand alone.

One word of warning: this is not the kind of book that tells you what's wrong with yourself and leaves you hanging there. You already know, deep down, what's wrong. This book tells you what to do to make it right. Take time out right now. Part of you is missing. It's time to collect the missing pieces. Turn the pages and begin.

1 JANUARY
I'm Good at Being Me

Life is not a having and a getting,
but a being and a becoming.
                    —Matthew Arnold

Sometimes I think that January 1 is the most important day of the year. Weather-wise, it might need a little improvement; *other*wise, the first day of January provides us all with the one thing we humans can't get along without: the chance for a new beginning.

We celebrate this chance in a thousand different ways. It's one of the oldest customs in the world. In ancient times, the new year was in the spring, because new crops meant a new beginning. Since South Pacific islanders enjoy warm weather all year long, they plant crops often. Every time they bury new seeds, they celebrate a new year. In Madagascar and Burma, people pour water on their heads to wash away their sins. In India, the Hindus bathe in the Ganges River. But the time of year is not as important as the idea of a fresh start.

Clean starts have been important since the very beginning. Something within each of us cries out for one more chance. We want, like the schoolchild who begs his teacher to let him erase the blackboard, to wipe the slate clean. We need to put our mistakes behind us and start again.

"Ring out the old, ring in the new." No matter how it's celebrated, the coming of the new year is a universal holiday. It calls for celebration. No matter what the date, the meaning is the same. It's time to burn your bridges behind you and start over.

It's also a time for promises. We humans instinctively feel the need for guidelines. We are list makers; unfortunately, we are also list losers. We write down

things we intend to do . . . and promptly forget about
them. I once knew a woman named Mary Thompson who
was a great list maker. "I like to write everything down,"
Mary confided. "Once I get it on paper, I can put it out of
my mind."

Isn't that exactly what happens when we write down
our resolutions? Good intentions are easily put away and
forgotten, unless . . . (1) we keep them simple and (2) we
do something about them *every single* day. The trouble
is, resolutions tend to be vague and unrealistic, like items
out of an overpriced wish book, and vague things quickly
become boring and easy to put off until later.

Listen closely! I'm going to show you how to stop all
this fooling around. Keep reading and find out how to
make two simple resolutions that will change your life.
They're unbelievably simple; you can do something about
them every day; most important, they cover all the bases.
Here they are:

1. Accept yourself as a child of God.
2. Let his will be your will.

My neighbor, Kate Goodwin, tells me that she always
gets up early on New Year's morning. No matter how
late she's stayed up the night before, she manages to
crawl out of bed before anyone else is stirring. She sits
alone at a table by the kitchen window, and she always
says aloud, "Here we go again, God. You and me and a
brand new year."

Intuitively, Kate has discovered the formula for a fresh
start. She has (1) accepted herself, and (2) joined hands
with God. It's as simple as that.

How do I know she's accepted herself? Look at her
words. Kate has obviously been there before. "Here we go
again," she says. She's tried, and made mistakes, but she
isn't giving up. She's a worthwhile enough person to
reach out and take God's hand and believe she can do
better next time. Kate knows she has faults, but she also
has potential; otherwise, there would be no point in
giving it another try.

That's all very well, you're thinking, but just how do *I*
go about this business of accepting *my*self. First, take a

good look at you. You know yourself better than **anybody** else, so be honest. What do you see? What do you do **all** day? What do you wish you were doing? What do you think about, laugh about, yearn for? What makes **you** happy, and what makes you sad? No matter what **your** answers, there is one basic fact you've got to **remember.** You are *somebody.* No matter what you do from **the time** you get up in the morning until you shut your **eyes at** night, you are a working woman. You have responsibilities, whether in an office, a schoolroom, **a** hospital, a community, or in your own home. What it **is** that you do has importance, and don't you forget it.

Carol Barker sat at the kitchen table looking wistfully out the window. She watched as her **neighbor** Millie backed the car out of the driveway and **drove** around the corner and out of sight. Carol spooned another mouthful of hot cereal into her youngest, **who** promptly blew it back out again and simultaneously overturned his cup of milk. Carol sighed. She still **had** three lunches to pack and the laundry to sort. She **stared** out the window again, remembering how fresh Millie **had** looked. "No wonder," she grumbled. "She *should* **look** wonderful. All she has to do is sit in a nice air-conditioned office all day."

By this time, Millie was pulling onto the freeway. **She** was going to be late again, and her boss would **be** anything but pleased. Everything had gone wrong **that** morning. There was a button missing on her blouse. **Her** scarf was in the wash. The shoulder strap had **broken on** her best white purse. She was still breathless **from** patching herself together and getting the children **off to** school. She actually felt queasy when she pulled **into the** parking lot. She had six extra reports to type **before** lunch, and she'd forgotten to take the casserole **out of the** freezer. A picture of Carol flashed through her **mind. She** had seen her sitting by the window feeding **the baby.** "That's the life," she murmured. "I wonder what **it's like** to stay home all day and do whatever you feel like."

Both viewpoints were backside-forward. Carol **and** Millie had evidently forgotten that the grass is *not* greener on the other side. Don't *you* make the same mistake. Don't worry about the way your neighbor spends her day. Think about what *you* do. Be proud of it. A person who downgrades her own role in life is standing on the bottom rung of the ladder.

Now that you know that you're somebody and have gained a little more self-respect, don't begin to think you're perfect. Liking yourself doesn't mean overlooking your handicaps. Look right at them instead. Face it, we are endowed with more than "certain inalienable rights." We are also endowed with certain inescapable equipment, some of it good, and some of it in need of improvement. Our handicaps are part of what we have to work with. In spite of them, or maybe because of them, our potential is unlimited. Helen Keller once said, "I thank God for my handicaps, for through them I have found myself, my work, and my God."

What if your handicap is some flaw in your personality? Perhaps you think that you're not a very likable person. You can respect your role in life, but you have a terrible time trying to learn to like yourself. Remember this: you may have problems, make mistakes, yell at your children, nag at your husband . . . but the real you . . . the one God intended you to be . . . *is* a likable person. That's what this book is all about.

Besides, you have no right to put yourself down. Let me tell you about Catherine Mason. She lives alone in a small apartment in a growing community near Los Angeles. Her home is immaculately clean. She spends all day every Saturday re-scrubbing and re-polishing. Catherine is an attractive, unmarried second-grade schoolteacher. She attends church, but makes no friends. People, she thinks, don't find her interesting. She is in her early thirties, but seldom attends social functions. She would rather sit home with a good book. "I am," she once told me, "not very good company." She looked down at her folded hands. "I'm really not a very remarkable person."

Catherine's attitude is beginning to affect her job. She is having discipline problems in class. She depends

entirely on teaching manuals and hasn't come up with
an original, creative idea for a long time. Why? Because
her self-respect is at an all-time low, and her students
sense this. If she doesn't respect herself, they're not going
to respect her either. She feels incapable of creativity and
growth.

The truth is, Catherine has put herself down so many
times, she believes what she says. She looks at herself
and she doesn't like what she sees. Sadly, she is
becoming that person she dislikes. Catherine has
forgotten one very important fact. She is a child of God.
Whatever he creates *is* remarkable. Whether she likes it
or not, Catherine Mason is a unique human being. She
has no right to put herself down. Neither have you!

Listen to another story. Janice Baker was a substitute
teacher in a large and difficult district. She was
consistently assigned to junior high classes in schools
with discipline problems. Janice rarely had problems
with her students, and one day she told me her secret.

"The first class I had was a horror," she said. "They
threw paper balls, shot rubber bands, and called me
'Teach'! Somehow I had to get their respect, or I was
through. So I stood in front of the class, with my hands
at my sides. And I repeated very quietly, at least five
times, three words. I said them slowly and very firmly.
They were, 'Look . . . at . . . me!' Slowly, but surely, they
looked. I let my eyes rest for a second on each face. Then
I said, insistently, 'I'm somebody. I have a name. Learn
it, and use it. I am your teacher for today, but I'm more
than that. I'm a particular teacher. I'm Miss Baker!' Then
before they could recover, I gave them their assignment.
I've never changed the procedure. It works every time."

Janice had simply been reaffirming the fact of her
uniqueness as a human being. She respected herself and
asked for respect from others. Here are a few rules to help
you carry out the first part of your resolution. By now
you should have taken a good look at yourself. You
should know that you are somebody and that, with all
your faults, God loves you the way you are. Here's how to
begin to accept yourself.

1. Learn to accept a compliment. Don't shake your head and look at the floor. Smile. Be gracious. Say thank you. It's really pretty insulting to deny a compliment. Someone was trying to say something nice about you. Why do you want to make a liar out of him?

2. At the beginning of each day, think of three things you know you can do well. Then plan to do them that day. Bake a cake. Arrange some flowers. Change the beds. Write a note to a sick friend. Make these things small enough so that you'll have plenty of time for them, then *do* them before the day is over. I know . . . we all have those days when nothing seems to go right, when we're sure there isn't anything at all we can do well. Even on days like those . . . *especially* on days like those . . . something redeeming will turn up.

Some time ago, I had a day like that. The alarm clock rang at 5:30 A.M., because our children had to catch the early schoolbus. I staggered out of bed, limped to the mirror, and took a good look. It wasn't what I wanted to see.

"Who are you?" I remember thinking. "What is your claim to fame?" Needless to say, it wasn't starting out to be the best of mornings. I went to the kitchen where I began stuffing sandwiches into brown paper bags. Through my window I could see that there was a world out there. But I was trapped. I was going to spend the rest of my life getting up at the crack of dawn and stuffing sandwiches into little paper bags. And who cared anyway? Who appreciated me?

I heard a noise behind me and turned to look at my youngest son, who was sitting on the stairs sleepily pulling on yesterday's socks. Before I could scold him and send him back for fresh ones, he asked a question.

"Why are you a mother?" he asked.

He caught me off guard. I had been thinking along those lines myself. "That's the way the world turns," I shrugged.

"I wouldn't be a mother for anything," he said.

I took a better look at him. "Seven years old," I

thought, "and he already has good sense." Then I got to thinking about it. "Why not?" I inquired.

"Because I can't make a fast peanut butter sandwich. Especially so early in the morning."

"What kind do you make?"

"Slow ones, but they don't taste so good. You have to be a mother to make a fast sandwich. If I didn't have a mother, I'd be stuck with slow sandwiches the rest of my life."

I looked out the window again. This time the sun was shining, and there was dew on the grass. But it was pretty nice in my kitchen too. My son had given me back a little self-respect at 6:00 in the morning. I remembered something my own mother had once said. "It isn't the sandwich that matters," she'd told me. "It's the stuffing that counts." Even peanut butter sandwiches can be an accomplishment when they're made with love.

3. Refuse to indulge in vicious gossip. This doesn't mean you can't ever talk about people. We talk *about* and *to* each other all the time. But watch out that you don't "put down" other people. It's the first sign of an "I don't like myself" complex, and we can't have any of that. After all, if you're unique, then your next door neighbor is too.

4. Celebrate something. Feel glad. Celebrate the rain, or celebrate the sunshine. In *Leaves of Grass* Walt Whitman said, "I celebrate myself . . ." Tell yourself you're a child of God, and celebrate *your* self. There is no vanity involved. Only joy and gratitude for life. You're not going out and telling everyone how wonderful you are. You're not trying to convince people of anything. You're just glad you're you. If there are things about yourself you'd like to change, make a list. Maybe you're overweight, or a chronic interrupter, or you drink too many cups of coffee. What you can change, change. What you can't change, accept. And don't forget to celebrate.

5. Remember the miracle at Cana. Christ changed water to wine. He did this sort of thing all the years he lived among us, constantly taking the common and

ordinary and making something special of it. Too often
we do the opposite. We reverse the miracle of Cana and
change wine back into water. Remember Cana and look
for the miracles of every day. Remember Cana and look
for the miracle of your own potential. What you are, can
be improved. If a silkworm, a plain little caterpillar, can
spin pure silk out of the very substance of its body, surely
you can spin a little silk out of the threads of your life.

6. When you make a mistake, force yourself to laugh.
Well, at least you can smile. Just because you have
learned some self-respect, don't let it go to your head. You
haven't become perfect. You'll make plenty more mistakes
before you're through. The difference is that if you can
smile, you won't go into a depression over a burned roast
or a missed appointment or a thoughtless deed. You learn
from the mistake, pick up the pieces, and take two giant
steps forward.

Now we come to the second part of your resolution: *Let
God's will be your will.* This is, perhaps, the most difficult
part of all, because we humans are pretty strong-willed
creatures ourselves. This is the only danger in learning to
accept yourself. You have to learn to recognize the
difference between self-confidence and vanity. So how
can you tell the difference between what he wants for you
and what you want for yourself? What *is* his will? How
do you *know*?

Listen, and he will tell you. I'm not talking about silent
prayer. Although meditation has a lot of value, you can't
go around meditating all day long. And that's when God
is talking to you. All day long. When you're making the
beds, when you're sweeping the porch, as you hold out
your hand to meet someone new, while you're rushing to
the supermarket trying to find something quick for
dinner, when you sit with your neighbor drinking a cup
of tea.

Don't wait for a booming voice to come thundering out
of the clouds. At least that's not the way God speaks to
me. Listen instead to your deepest feelings. Are you
someone who hangs back when you know you should

step forward? Do you feel strongly about something in
your community, but you hesitate, because you're afraid
to rock the boat? Do you stay away from a house in
mourning, because you don't know how to offer comfort?

Now hold on! I'm not suggesting that you become a
compulsive doorbell ringer. I'm not telling you to run out
and join every committee in town. I'm saying that you
should stop ignoring that still, small voice that we all
hear from time to time. Here's how:

1. Don't stifle all your impulses. If you're thinking
about an old friend who lives on the other side of town,
don't just sit there. Call her up and tell her you miss her.
Smile at the stranger waiting next to you in line. When
you ask someone, "How are you?" mean it . . . and listen
attentively to the answer. When your family talks to you,
listen to more than their words. Let intuition be your guide.
Feel their deepest needs. React to the sounds of their
voices. Hear what it is they're *really* trying to tell you.

2. Listen for the signals of change. Don't say, "Sorry,
but that's the way I am." Especially if you know the way
you are is the wrong way. You won't be the same "you"
every day of your life anyway. There is no excuse to do
less than your best at today's job, but how many times
today did you have a chance to do something in a
different way? How many opportunities opened up? How
many new ideas popped into your head? Try something
new every day, even if it's only a new recipe. That new
chance you turned down may have been the fresh start
you were looking for.

All of us go through cycles of change. We are growing,
developing human beings. The direction you take as you
grow and develop will determine what you do with the
rest of your life. Start now by accepting yourself as a
child of God and deciding that you want his will to be
your will. Start every day of the month of January by
repeating the old Quaker proverb: "Today is the first day
of the rest of my life." Celebrate a fresh start every
morning. Celebrate yourself . . . and listen for direction. It
will come.

Thank you, Lord, for the gift of myself.
Let me accept what you have given;
Take my hand and show me your will.
Help me, Lord, to spin a little silk
With the threads of my life.

2 FEBRUARY
Only Dogs Chase Their Tails

To see a world in a grain of sand
And a heaven in a wildflower:
Hold infinity in the palm of your hand,
And eternity in an hour.
—William Blake

What do *you* do with an hour? Do you sense that precious piece of eternity that is here, then gone so quickly? Do you value it and use it, knowing that you'll never have another chance to use it again? Or do you open your fingers and let infinity dribble out like unnoticed grains of sand?

It's February . . . the shortest month of the year. That means we have less hours to fool around with than usual. It also means that we've come to the best month of the year to start talking about time and how you use it.

In recent years researchers have been involved in a unique study called garbageology. That's right, they collect garbage. They sort it, and study it, and find out all about the people who throw it away. It's amazing, they tell me, how much you can learn about a person from the things he throws in the trash. It's like a kind of living archaeology, only they don't have to dig as deep for their information.

How do *you* feel about letting people learn about you by studying what you throw away? Or . . . worse yet . . . by looking at how much you waste? I for one don't much like the idea. But I think that the idea of garbageology goes far beyond the trash can. What about wasted time? It's one of the most precious things we have, and we are more careless with our time than with anything else we throw away.

The pressure of time . . . the lack of it . . . is one of life's major sources of stress. All of us seem to have one thing in common: too much to do and not enough time in which to do it. Work itself is not really the problem. As a matter of fact, it's pretty good medicine. Frustration is the culprit to watch out for, and frustration is what occurs when you find yourself going around in circles.

It's cute when a puppy chases his tail. It's funny when a grown dog does it. But it's not even amusing when humans get caught like spinning tops, going round and round with no end in sight but dizziness.

How can you tell if you're a tail chaser? Ask yourself these questions: (1) Do you ever wake up in the morning full of enthusiasm but go to bed that night feeling like you've wasted a day? (2) Do you ever lie awake at night, worrying about the things that face you tomorrow? (3) Do you make promises, then wish you hadn't? (4) Do you hurry through easy jobs first and save the big ones until you have enough time to do them right? (5) Do you have more than one unfinished project waiting for you right now?

If you answered yes to any one of these questions, you could use a little more organization in your life. If you said yes to two or more, you had better read this chapter carefully, because you are on a merry-go-round, and, unless you change your ways, you're not going to catch the golden ring. What I'm trying to tell you is: *you're not getting a free ride*. People who go around in circles pay and pay and pay again.

I can already hear you protesting. "But I'm *working!*" you insist. "I don't sit around wasting my time. It's not my fault that I have too much to do."

Yes it is. If you have too much to do, you've either taken on more than you can handle, or you're a time waster. Either way, it's your fault, isn't it? You need to ask yourself two questions.

(1) What are you really accomplishing?

(2) What do you really want to accomplish?

If you're being honest with yourself, you'll recognize the fact that you're getting nowhere fast, because you're going through life like the man who quit his job and wandered all over the world without a road map. He saw a lot of countryside. Sometimes he saw it twice. But he never got anywhere, because he couldn't decide where he was going.

How hard you work every day doesn't have anything to do with it. Work without some kind of goal is about as sensible as dieting when you're already skinny. There just isn't any purpose to it. You may see lots of countryside: you may see some of it twice. But you'll never get anywhere, because you haven't decided where you're going, and you don't even have a road map.

Don't be like Sara Cunningham, who started out to plant a bed of pansies. It wasn't a particularly large project. She needed to do a little weeding, add some fertilizer to the soil, then set out the plants and water them. The whole process should have taken a couple of hours. Her goal was what? A bed of pansies? That's what you think!

Sara spread that job over a two-week period, working at the plot an inch at a time and talking incessantly about how much work it was. At the end of each day she would give a deep sigh. Really, she told herself, I am a very busy person. When the ground was finally ready, she decided to plant tomatoes instead. She thought a fence would be nice for them to climb on. She'd paint it white and expand the garden. She made a lot of plans. Pretty soon it was too late in the season to plant anything at all.

Sara is the perfect example of someone who expands her work to fill up her time. Work, for Sara, is an end, not a means to an end. She needs to appear busy in order to appear important to herself. She is a tail chaser, because she never moves forward in a straight line. A little side-tracking is normal. It can even be productive. But circles get you nowhere.

How, then, do you break the cycle? How do you go about sorting out your goals? How do you clean up the disorder of your life? That's exactly what I'm going to tell you. Disorder can start anywhere at all. It feeds upon itself like a hungry animal, and it can't be stopped *from the outside*. That's because order starts *on the inside*. The inside of YOU. It starts with basics. What you need is simplification, not more complication. You have to get *yourself* organized, before you start on the world. You have to get a road map before you can find your way around town.

Transcendental Meditation, ladies, that over-promoted, but very popular panacea, is not the answer. It's supposed to take the disorder out of your mind, leaving you refreshed and ready to tackle the world. It involves a process in which you are supposed to repeat over and over your very own secret "mantra," which happens to be meaningless unless you speak Sanskrit. All the better, I'm told, because knowing the meaning would only distract you anyway. A session of TM is supposed to relax and refresh, sending you running back into the stream of things with your tensions released and your body renewed. I have news for you. Your problems are right out there waiting for you, just like the proverbial breakfast dishes. You may feel relaxed, and your mind may be emptied of all its frustrations. But a hot bath would have relaxed you just as well, and who needs an empty mind, anyway?

I'm not telling you that meditation is no good. It is. Quiet moments are always of value. I *am* telling you that no amount of meditation will get your piled-up work done for you. The danger in depending on something like TM is that it can become a closet to hide in.

The only way to stop going around in circles is facing up to what you have to do each day. And the way you face up to each day is to approach it one step at a time. The way I do this is by writing everything down.

That's right. I'm talking about list-making. Don't shake your head and turn away. List-making has been around for a long time. I think it was probably one of man's (and woman's) earliest occupations. If you don't want to take a tip from me, take a tip from Santa, the greatest list-maker of them all. Don't you remember? He was always "making a list and checking it twice . . ."?

The list you make won't be like Santa's, because you're going to check it more than twice. You're going to work with it all day long. It's going to turn into a schedule. If you don't think you need one, try this:

Take a piece of paper and jot down every single thing you think you have to do today. I mean *everything*. Start from the time you get up in the morning and continue until you fall in bed at night. Include making the beds, writing letters, paying bills, picking up the house, shopping, mending, appointments, meetings, the time it takes you to go from one place to another in the car. You name it. Put it all down on paper. By the side of each item write down the approximate number of minutes that job will take to complete, and don't say twenty minutes when you know perfectly well that something takes at least half an hour. Are you finished? Add eight hours for sleeping, and be sure to include time for meals and coffee breaks. Add it all up. I'll bet you come up with a forty-eight-hour day.

Now if you're the kind of person who's saying, "I'm just not the kind of woman who can live by a schedule," I say to you, "Don't be so silly!"

No one is telling you to live by a schedule. A schedule is something you use! How can you be creative or whole or peaceful or anything else if your sink is full of dirty dishes and the bathroom needs scrubbing? Now I hope I don't offend anyone . . . and believe me, my house needs cleaning as often as anyone's . . . but the women I know who live in chaos while they paint beautiful pictures, and see the world through dirty windows, have as many hang-ups as the women who clean and scrub and dust so compulsively that they never have time or strength to see a sunset or hear a robin sing.

God did not mean for us to live in filth. Neither did he mean for us to scrub sinks all day. He meant for us to become whole human beings. Time is his gift to us, and we don't use it well while we're bound by daily frustrations and aggravations. Think of it this way: when you're wasting time, you're wasting a gift from God.

So stop wasting any more of it, and start making that

list. I'm going to show you how. The first thing for you to
do is to take a good look at one single day. No more. For
the time being, don't think about yesterday or tomorrow.
Today is all you have to work with. Take a fresh piece of
paper and divide it into three vertical sections. At the top
of the first section write the words, "Have to." In this
column list all the things that you consider absolutely
necessary . . . the things that absolutely have to be done
on that day. Use that forty-eight-hour day of yours as a
guide. Don't put on this list anything that you can
possibly put off until tomorrow.

Next, at the top of the center column write the words,
"Should Do." These are those things you've been putting
off, and could probably put off a little longer. Things like
scrubbing the pantry shelves or cleaning the medicine
cabinet or answering letters. Put some things on this list
that only take fifteen minutes or so to complete. Like
sweeping the porch or straightening one drawer. You're
more likely to make a stab at one of them if they don't
take too much time.

Third, jot down a couple of "Wish I Coulds," like
reading, or playing the piano, or painting your toenails,
or taking a walk. These sit by themselves in the right-
hand column like peppermint candies at the end of
dinner. Think of them as treats. Think of them as
rewards. But don't touch them unless you deserve them.

You've got the picture. First come the necessaries. You
have to finish all of those. Then choose at least one of the
should dos. You know what? You're going to have time
for one of those things you've always wished you had
time for. And you won't be as tired as usual, because you
didn't waste precious energy wondering where you were
going next.

Make a new list every night before you go to bed.
There's only one catch. Every item that you did not
complete on the old list has to be transferred to the new
list, and it has to remain there until you take a stab at it.
In other words, your have tos will always get done; your
should dos will eventually get done. And you'll have a
better chance of getting at those wishes if you keep

looking at them. That schedule you thought you were going to hate is exactly what is going to make you free, because you've organized yourself so that you're no longer chasing your tail.

It's very important for you to keep a family calendar, the kind that has a place for you to write under each date. Then you'll always have a record of monthly obligations to transfer daily to your schedule. When you're making your new list every night, try to keep four things in mind.

1. Don't make promises that you can't keep. Recognize your own limitations as well as your priorities. If something is going to get shuffled to the bottom of your should do list day after day, it probably shouldn't have been put there in the first place.

2. Don't spread yourself too thin. This isn't an endurance contest. You must figure out exactly how much you are able to do in one given day and not feel guilty about the rest. All of us are human. We all get tired. We all change our minds.

3. Leave a little room for spontaneity. Whatever you do, don't fill up your day completely. Leave at least one whole hour tucked away somewhere. If you don't have to use it, it's all yours for a "wish I could." Once in a while, do something unconventional. Are you a creature of habit? If you wake up early in the morning, do you lie there for an hour waiting for the alarm to ring? Get up instead and enjoy one early hour all by yourself. If you're not sleepy at night, do you lie there cursing the bad luck of insomnia? Turn on the light and read a book. Get up and bake a cake. Who says you can't?

Haven't you ever felt like taking a little time off? Sometimes you've done just that. You settled down with a good book, or climbed into the car, or started off on a long walk. Then you came back and looked at all there still was to do, and you felt guilty about it. What was your next step? Why, you jumped right in there and tried to make up for lost time, didn't you? You chased your tail harder than ever, and you got nowhere fast. You made one basic mistake. You didn't make your schedule flexible

enough. You wouldn't have felt guilty about enjoying
something that was part of your master plan.

4. Don't confuse your goals with someone else's. Decide
what's important to you, and stick with it. Let me give
you an example.

When our four children were very small, I had a friend
who swept her front porch before she did anything else in
the morning. The first time I saw her wielding her broom
was on a windy November day. It was 7:00 A.M., and I
was just venturing out the front door to bring in the milk.
I rubbed my eyes and stared across the street.

"Mildred," I called. "Is that you?"

A swirl of dried leaves rose in the air and settled back
defiantly into place. "Of course, it's me," she replied
grimly.

"Why are you fighting those leaves at seven o'clock in
the morning?"

"Because it's the way I start my day." She shook a
finger at me. "Never underestimate the importance of
your porch," she admonished. "People look at it and
know all about you. Why, your porch is a reflection of the
rest of your house. A woman with dirt on her doormat is
a woman with dust balls under her beds."

I glanced around sheepishly and went into the house.
Three cups of coffee later, I'd mustered enough courage to
go back and look again. My front porch was still there.
So were four bikes, a rake with no handle, a tire pump, a
box of leaves, two dogs, one cat, and several children, not
all of them mine. On the front door handle swung an
inner tube.

"Why are you smiling like that?" asked my young son.

"Because at least there isn't any dirt on the doormat," I
told him. Cleaning the front porch was on my list for the
day, but it came beneath baking cookies for the children,
which was a promise I intended to keep. I was taking the
last batch out of the oven when the doorbell rang.

It was Mildred. She wasn't staring at the leaves. My
front porch was just as I had left it, except that a large
tent made from old sheets and a broken lawn chair had
been added. There was also a lot of noise. From under the

tent came a voice, off-key, but singing. Somebody giggled. The dog howled. The cat stretched lazily and watched a curious bird. Three beautiful scarlet leaves drifted slowly down and settled at my feet.

Mildred was right, I thought. People can look at your front porch and know all about you.

"I don't know how you can look so pleased with yourself," she burst out. "Why, if my porch looked like this, I know what *I'd* be doing."

I knew too. I smiled at her and held out the plate. "Have a cookie," I said.

Mildred's priorities were hers, and mine were mine. Neither of us was wrong. Later in the morning I cleaned the porch, and quite possibly Mildred baked some cookies. So don't judge your neighbor on the basis of what you think she *ought* to be doing. And don't worry if she judges you. We all make our own lists. We each see a different world in a grain of sand.

When you know what *your* goal is at the end of each day, when you make a schedule that guides you like a road map, then you'll have the peace of mind to recognize that precious piece of eternity in every hour. And you'll stop going around in circles. After all, only dogs chase their tails.

Thank you, Lord, for the gift of time.
Show me how to use each moment of eternity,
Wasting not . . . but spending wisely.
Help me, Lord, to recognize
Important things. Help me to choose wisely,
Facing each day with confidence and anticipation.

3 MARCH
No Is a Positive Word

One man with courage makes a majority.
—Andrew Jackson

*. . . the lamentable difficulty I have always
experienced in saying "No."*
—Coleridge

I always think of March as a month with a mind of
its own. I wish I could say the same for a lot of people.
Sometimes I think that we humans are made like those
little spring-necked dolls that sit in the back windows of
cars and in carnival stalls. They nod their heads at the
least excuse, and that's the only motion they can make.
Nudge them, jiggle them, blow on them, and their heads
start bobbing mindlessly up and down.

March is not a mindless month. It's full of vigor and
strength. When I was a small child, an elderly neighbor,
who was popularly known as "Uncle," used to go outside
every morning and sniff the air. I mean *really* sniff it!
He'd throw back his shoulders, hold his head high, place
his feet far apart, lift his hands slightly, palms forward,
and BREATHE. When he was finished, he'd give his
opinion freely to anyone who wanted to hear it.

I remember it was the first day of March, and I was in
the front yard when he came out of his house one day
and sniffed suspiciously. "Well, now," he said and sniffed
again. Then he gave a broad smile. "That's more like it,"
he told me. "March air. It gives a man the courage of his
convictions."

I didn't know what he was talking about then, but I do
now. March is a wonderful month for breathing deeply
and soaking up a little courage. It's the perfect time for
strengthening convictions. It's full of thirty-one wonderful

days, and you can use every one of them to develop a mind of *your* own.

The first thing you need is a little courage. Because you're going to learn to say "No." And it isn't an easy word to say. Isn't that negative thinking? Not at all. Saying no doesn't mean you're anti-positive. As a matter of fact, a compulsive head nodder doesn't think positively. He doesn't even think negatively. He doesn't think at all.

You can't always go through life nodding your head and smiling pleasantly. So much has been said in recent years about the value of having a positive attitude, that we've been just a little bit brainwashed into believing that anything else is wrong. Watch out! You can get into a whole lot of trouble by nodding your head.

A close friend of mine . . . call her Mary Johnson . . . refused to admit what was growing obvious to every one else. Mary was losing her hearing. It was simpler, she thought, to smile and nod her way through a conversation than to admit she couldn't hear what was going on. Not only did she look pretty silly, but she made dates she didn't keep and found herself in an important position on a Democratic women's organization. That wouldn't have been so bad, except that Mary was a staunch Republican.

A lot of us nod and smile, just like Mary, even though we have perfect hearing. Remember this: our necks are made so that our heads can move in almost all directions. Sometimes it is necessary to move them from side to side.

Young children don't have any difficulty with this movement at all. Saying no is no problem for them. Even babies love the word, and they don't have any inhibitions about it. Listen to any child say no. Hear that sound of authority? It comes out loud and clear. It may distress their mothers, but at least little children are not afraid to shake their heads.

As we get a little older, popularity becomes important. We want to be liked. It's easier to go along with the crowd. It's more pleasant to agree than to disagree. Gradually, but persistently, we become nodders.

In our adult years we want respect. We need to show others how capable we are; we want to believe we're indispensable. So we pile on more and more responsibility. You've all heard the advice, "If you want to get something done, ask the busiest person in town to do it." I used to think that was a compliment. Now I'm not so sure. If you've earned the title of "busiest person" and people call on you continually for just one more job, maybe it's time for you to learn a new head movement.

Life, you know, is full of decisions. Just when you think you've found the soft place in the mattress, a bump appears. Something comes up that forces you to make some kind of adjustment. Change is like the yeast that makes a loaf of bread rise. Without it, we might as well live on flat soda crackers. New choices and new commitments are part of facing each day. And *you have to make them.* Whether you like it or not, you can't go through life without getting off the fence. Oh, you might manage to stay up there awhile. You might even get pretty comfortable. But if you know what's good for you, you had better climb down before you fall. There's always a strong wind when you least expect it. Make your decision and jump before it blows you somewhere you don't want to go.

What has all this got to do with shaking your head? I'll tell you. So much is said about doing, and being, and becoming . . . that we neglect to lift up the pancake and see what's happening on the other side. Deciding what you're going to *do* about something necessitates putting certain things behind you. You also have to decide what you're *not* going to do. Sometimes this deciding requires a shake of the head. Refusing something that isn't good for you . . . coming right out and saying no . . . is a positive assertion that you're in control of your own best interests.

Our best example is the Man who stood in the wilderness and denied temptation (Matthew 4: 1-10). Christ was saying, "No. I can't. I won't." And in his denial . . . in his negative reaction . . . he *affirmed* his positive relationship with God.

What's *your* relationship with God? Next time the

opportunity arises (and it will, this very day) for you to
say no to things that you know are wrong for you . . . do
it! Say no! Say no to the dessert you shouldn't eat. Say no
to the committee you shouldn't belong to. Say no to your
child, even when it would be easier to say yes. Say no
about something important. Watch what happens. How
do you feel? Relief? A sense of well-being? The ability to
move forward in another direction? Peace of mind,
because you're sure you've made the right decision?
That's what I call a positive reaction!

Think of NO as a red light. Highway traffic would be
in a snarl without stop signs. So would your health.
Luckily, your body has an automatic red light system
that activates automatically.

Jane Anderson was a workaholic. She got up early and
organized her day down to the last ten details that she
could squeeze into the last five minutes. She went to bed
as late as she could, wishing that she could find some
way of organizing her sleep. She attended meetings,
cleaned her house, entertained, took the children to
scouts, sports, and dentist appointments. Let's face it.
Jane was a whiz. She was one of a kind, and everyone
knew it. "When you were made," people told her,
"someone broke the mold." Jane smiled brightly and
joined another committee.

One day she opened her eyes and discovered she
couldn't get out of bed. She couldn't understand it. She'd
never been sick a day in her life. But for some reason, her
muscles seemed to have turned to jelly.

The doctor diagnosed her condition. "I could give you a
long medical term," he told her, "but complete exhaustion
is what you've got. Your body rebelled. You pushed it
until it finally had to say no."

Jane Anderson isn't unique. When *you* overdo, when
you're exhausted, *your* body also says "NO!" You're
finally forced to do something about it. You have to go
rest, don't you? Even if it's against your will, you're
forced to stop for the red light. You're forced to take some
action. And it's a positive action, because it's leading
toward positive results. But you had to start out by

saying no. The word is like a safety valve. Without it, we would just keep on storing up steam until we burst.

You can rush around nodding your head all you want, but all the positive action in the world won't get you to the moon, if you run out of gas between here and the airport. You need a rest stop . . . the pause that refreshes . . . you need to say, "Hey, wait a minute. Stop, and let me get my breath."

Ruby Emerson, a remarkable woman of sixty-five, told me that she wished she hadn't waited so long to discover the value of the word no. "Look at me," she said. "I'm sixty-five years old, and what have I accomplished? A lifelong series of committee chairmanships. People kept after me until I said yes, because it was easier than explaining why I wanted to say no. I knew I was taking on too many extra activities. I was gone from home too much when my children needed me. I almost wore out the can opener, and I came close to exhausting my husband's patience. I ended up actually resenting a lot of the jobs I got roped into."

If Ruby made so many mistakes, why do I call her remarkable? Because she has determined to change. Victor Hugo once said that if you wanted to reform a man, you would have to start with his grandmother. Ruby Emerson says, "Fiddlesticks to that!"

"To reform anyone," she told me, "you have to start with that person and start right now. That's what I'm doing. I'm even practicing in the mirror every morning. I'm looking at myself and shaking my head and forcing myself to keep a pleasant expression on my face. I'm refusing with a smile. Isn't it a shame," she added, "that I waited so long to take control of my own decisions?"

Ruby has learned something important. It's possible to say no without being offensive about it. But it takes a little practice. You have to learn to smile while you're doing it. Unfortunately, it's a little like rubbing your head and patting your stomach at the same time.

But you can do it now. You *can* be pleasant, and you *can* be firm. The next time you find yourself in a difficult situation and want out, give a great big smile and shake

your head. You'll be surprised how little argument you
get in return.

Here's something to think about. Every one of the
Ten Commandments except two are negative. They tell
us what not to do. Life is made up of dos *and* don'ts. You
have to learn to use them both with discretion. Too much
salt ruins the meal. Too much pepper makes your tongue
burn.

It's not too late to take your life by the reins.
Sometimes, in order to stop yourself from going over the
cliff, you have to stop and change gears. Think positive!
Act positive! Pray positive! Never let the ideal that you're
striving for slip out of your mind. But remember that you
sometimes have to say no to get those positive results.
Here are ten rules to help you.

1. Every morning, before you bring in the paper, or put
on the coffee, open the door (or window) and breathe.
Really breathe. Throw your arms wide . . . hold your head
high . . . and let the fresh strong air of March fill your
lungs. Then say to yourself, "Today, I'll be honest with
myself."

2. Remember that to deny is not to reject. Know the
difference.

3. Give a direct answer to a direct question. Don't be
afraid to say no to a child. It can be a healthy reaction to
a bad situation. Face it, your offspring aren't always
angels. You can love them and still say no.

4. Realize that no is only negative when it's a cop-out.
This keeps you from being ashamed to say no to an
adult. You're not withdrawing from responsibility. You're
re-directing it.

5. Analyze your feelings. Look on the other side of the
pancake. If you're feeling negative, look for the positive
reaction, then move forward.

6. Never say no, when you mean yes. Never say yes,
when you mean no. Make up your mind. You're the only
one who can.

7. Don't nag. Say it once and mean it. Nagging is like
a drop of acid. Sometimes the damage is not immediately
apparent. At first, there's only a slight stain on the cloth.

Then one day a hole appears. The result: a complete void in place of something of value.

8. Practice this positive statement: "Yes, I'm saying no!"

9. Learn to smile pleasantly when you shake your head. Scowls only make wrinkles, and there's nothing positive about those.

10. Take a tip from Ruby Emerson and start reforming today. Start again *every* day for the whole month of March.

Does it sound like a lot to remember? It won't be as hard as you think, because God is right there waiting at every turn of the road. So stop coasting and get yourself in gear. Have the courage of your convictions. You know what kind of person God intended you to be. Don't settle for less.

Help me, Lord, to forsake mindlessness.
Give me the courage to use my voice
To deny what I know is wrong.
Give me the strength to shake my head,
And turn my feet another way.
Let me move forward with an unburdened heart.

4 APRIL
How Does Your Garden Grow?

*Now 'tis the spring, and
   weeds are shallow rooted;
Suffer them now and they'll o'er-
   grow the garden.*
—Shakespeare: *King Henry VI,*
                                    Part II

April has always been the traditional month for spring housecleaning. I'm not sure where the habit got started, but I suspect that it's some kind of natural reaction. Women all over the world smell spring in the air, promptly throw open their doors, wash their windows, and clean out their cupboards.

That's undoubtedly why there are so many rummage sales in the spring of the year. I recently heard one woman complain about the timing. "We should wait and have these sales just before the Christmas holidays," she said. "That's when everybody is in a buying mood."

The woman in charge of the next booth laughed. "Maybe you're right, Myra, but I wouldn't be in a cleaning mood then. I feel like cleaning things out in the spring. And once I get started, I want to get rid of all my piles of junk. I don't want to save them until the end of the year."

I think she had a good point and a healthy attitude. Junk is depressing. So is clutter. Why save it? As a matter of fact, why wait until spring to get rid of it? Let's see what the experts say.

A couple of years ago I read a report that made a startling claim. "Spring housecleaning," it stated, "is out of style. The modern woman cleans as she goes and no longer bothers to turn her house inside out once a year. The

annual wall washings and rug beatings are a thing of
the past."

That's pretty heady stuff. But wait a minute before you
swallow the sugar-coated pill. I'll admit that there's a lot
to be said for cleaning as you go. And as far as rug
beating goes . . . it can go as far as it likes. But I also
think there's a lot to be said for turning things inside out
once in a while. There's something invigorating about
open windows, furniture polish, and fresh paper on the
cupboard shelves. It's wonderful to be able to look around
and see the whole thing in order.

My grandmother used to say, "Don't be ashamed of
wielding a dust mop. Spring housecleaning is good for
your soul." Why spring? Because that's when you *can*
throw open your doors and clear away the cobwebs. It's a
time of sunshine and fresh air, not dust and dark corners.

So go ahead and be old-fashioned. Use the month of
April to put in order the physical world around you. Open
up *your* closets and cupboards. Wipe them clean. Discard
what you'll never use again. Start with one room at a far
corner of the house, and work your way through every
drawer and cubbyhole. Wash the walls, attack the spider
webs, shine the windows! Vacuum . . . dust . . . polish. If
cleanliness is really next to godliness, you'll be right at
the top of the list!

Don't let the job overwhelm you. Do it a step at a time.
Set your house in order, and *you* will be in control of the
things in it. It's good practice for what's coming next, for
the month of April is good for much more than cleaning
house.

In April the flowering nectarines bloom, soft and pink
against stiff gray branches. Wisteria blossoms fall,
silently coating the ground with a lavender carpet, like
ripe grapes drying in the sun. Roses bloom, trees turn
green. The ground warms, and thousands of bulbs open
and work their way through the soil toward the sun.

Other things grow too. We call them weeds. Some are
fragile and easy to get rid of, but others are tenacious,
with deep roots and tough stems. You're not a good
gardener if you let them grow. It's a good idea, once a

year, to take stock and use some spring housecleaning
techniques in your garden. Cast off the worn-out and
worthless. Weed out the cupboards of your garden, and
make room for fresh new life.

The idea is as old as Mother Goose. Remember the old
nursery rhyme: "Mary, Mary, quite contrary, how does
your garden grow?" I used to think it was talking about
tulips and daffodils. But a few years ago, I had second
thoughts.

It was during a period of my life when our four
children were young and demanding, my husband
worked long hours and traveled a lot, and I was involved
in so many time-consuming things that I never seemed to
have enough hours to finish the day's chores. With the
exhausting schedule I followed, I should have fallen into
bed at night and slept without a thought in my head.

But that's not the way it was. More and more I found
myself lying there at night, staring at the ceiling. I was
wide awake, and that's the way I stayed. Somehow, all
the things that seemed normal in the sunlight grew and
became distorted, until little worries and silly fears
became monsters, stretching across my mind like
shadows in the darkness.

Some people call it insomnia. My neighbor, Carol, had
another name for it. She dropped by one morning while I
was huddled over the coffee pot, trying to forget another
sleepless night.

"You look terrible!" she exclaimed. "Is anything
wrong?"

"I just couldn't sleep last night."

"Maybe you're too tired," she said. "Or maybe you're
worrying about something."

I avoided her eyes and reached for a cup. I didn't want
anyone to know about the monsters that visited me after
dark. "Not really," I hedged. "It's . . . well, it's just a lot
of silly little things." I started to pour some coffee into
her cup, but she stopped me.

"Not now. This morning I'm weeding the yard, and I'd
better get to work." She paused a second, then went on,
"You might try a little weeding yourself."

I stared at her, open-mouthed. My yard needed work, but it wasn't in bad enough shape for the neighbors to tell me about it. She must have read my thoughts. "I'm not talking about your yard," she laughed. "I'm talking about your mind. The real reason you didn't sleep last night was because you were so busy cultivating."

"Cultivating?"

"That's what I said. Cultivating your mind. The only trouble is, you were growing weeds up there instead of flowers."

"I can't help it if I'm a worrier," I insisted.

"Sure you can. All you have to do is pull out the bad thoughts, one by one."

I looked at her skeptically.

"You don't have to take my word for it," she shrugged. "But I've been there, and it worked for me. Why not try it?"

So I did. That first night was not a success. I tossed and turned for two or three hours. By then I was on the road to nowhere, and I knew it. So I closed my eyes and forced myself to concentrate on one single, worrisome, negative thought. Then I reached in mentally and pulled it out, just like a weed. I didn't tuck it away either, to pull out and examine later. I told myself I was through with that worry . . . permanently.

It wasn't easy. Those weeds were rooted deep, and they were stubborn. They kept trying to reseed. The only way I could stop them was to quickly fill each empty spot in my mind with something pleasant, the most pleasant thought possible, concentrating on it hard and letting my mind surround it until it filled my thoughts.

Then, it was morning, and I had slept soundly. More important, I had learned that fertile soil is found in more places than the backyard. It can just as easily nourish a weed patch as a garden. It all depends upon the gardener.

After that, pulling weeds became a habit. I found I could do it while running the vacuum, pushing a grocery cart, or cooking dinner. Every time one of the ugly little fellows reared his head and tried to clutter up my mind, I just reached in mentally and jerked him out.

At first, it took a lot of self-discipline, but it got easier as time went on. Then something strange began to happen. I seemed to be more efficient, to get chores done quicker, and I wasn't as tired at the end of the day.

One day a friend said, "You seem so different. So relaxed. Don't you ever worry about anything?"

I could only smile. For I had discovered that there is a big difference between worry and concern. I was still concerned about things, but I was learning to put triteness in its proper place, at the bottom of the compost pile, where it could sputter and go out.

I also learned that if I pulled weeds every night, the soil was miraculously clean in the morning. It was like a fresh start every time I opened my eyes. Sure, there were still problems, some of them big ones. That's part of life. The secret in dealing with them, is not letting them deal with you.

Any good gardener will tell you that you have a choice. You can let the weeds sprout and multiply. You can stand by helplessly as they choke the life out of your flowers. Or you can cultivate the garden of your mind, and watch your days bloom one by one.

Now wait a minute. Are you a little worried about those bare spots? Maybe weeding seems pretty easy, but re-seeding is out of your reach. Are you wondering exactly how to find something pleasant to fill the vacancies left by uprooted weeds? Let me tell you a story.

A ranger in the California Department of Forestry was inspecting the area devastated by a forest fire the year before. It was desolate . . . barren. The soil was black. The smell of charred wood still hung in the air. He shook his head. The whole terrain looked pretty bad. What could possibly grow there again?

It was early in April when he returned to the site to have another look at the damage, which he had considered total. To his amazement he saw soft green clumps of young grass and, among them, tall, slender stalks, covered with brilliant yellow flowers. He had seldom seen the Padre's Staff (*oenothera leptocarpa*), but he recognized it at once, and remembered that its seeds would only germinate after they were affected by intense heat, then rain. It had taken a forest fire to bring them to life.

You don't have to use measures that drastic. But the story applies to *you*. Don't be concerned about your new replacement thoughts. Just as new spring grass covers the barren hillside, so will new thoughts fill the barren places in your mind. Some varieties may have been lying there for years, wanting to be discovered. Wait until you recognize the one you want, then reach in and mentally plant it. Use your imagination. Use your memory. Use your dreams for the future. You'll be surprised at how many seed packets you come up with.

Now that you know all about weeding and re-seeding your garden, don't think you've come to the end of the story. Cultivation is important. But even a well-weeded garden can produce plants that don't look quite right. The leaves are pale; the blossoms droop. Because the garden hasn't been fed. Weed it, seed it, then feed it. That should be your motto.

I almost hate to make the following comparison, but it's a fact that fertilizer and faith have an awful lot in common. Fertilizer is plant food. Faith is soul food. Without fertilizer, your garden won't flourish. Without faith, your spirit won't grow. When plants are underfed, they droop. So do people. That's when we say someone has a case of the blues. Depression . . . dejection . . . downheartedness . . . you know the words. There are at least a dozen more, and they all mean the same thing. You're feeling low, and you can't seem to pull yourself out of the pit you've lowered yourself into.

That's what *you* think! You *can* cure the blues, but you need a foolproof method. What I'm going to tell you isn't painful; it doesn't cost a cent. It takes only five to ten minutes of your precious time. And you can do it in an easy-to-remember, step-by-step process.

1. Wash your face. Steam it with hot water, and splash it with cold. Do it again. Don't laugh. It's a fact that this process speeds up your circulation and makes you look better too. If you wear makeup, apply it carefully. You may feel low, but you're going to look *great*. Say to yourself that you're feeling better by the minute. You can see that you are *looking* better. All through? Now smile. Recent studies show that smiling may actually help you feel better. It may be even more effective than thinking happy thoughts. Try it. Force yourself to smile. It's hard to think glum, isn't it? Frown and see the difference.

2. Eat something. This is not the time to break your diet or gorge yourself on chocolate candy. This is the time for a nutrition break. Chances are you skipped a meal today anyway. So have a light snack right now, even if it's only a glass of milk. Temporary low blood sugar is easily and quickly remedied, and it's one of the major causes of feeling down in the dumps.

3. Treat yourself to a faith lift. Open your Bible to Matthew and read chapter 17, verse 20. The disciples came to Jesus and asked why they had been unable to heal others. They felt like failures. Is that the way you feel today? You're low and depressed, because things aren't going right. For some reason, you can't seem to get with it. There are too many problems to solve, and you don't feel capable of handling them.

"Why?" you ask. "Why am I a failure? Why am I making these mistakes? Why can't I do better?" If that's the way you feel, you're not the first. There's an answer for you, just as there was for the disciples. "It's because of your little faith," Jesus said. You don't have enough of it. With faith, nothing is impossible. What a tremendous promise! It's so tremendous, it's hard to comprehend.

How are you going to apply it to your problems today? How are you going to reach out for an idea that grand, while you're sitting there wallowing in depression? You're going to put things in perspective, that's how. Really now, how big are your problems? Even if they're pretty tremendous, do you need to move mountains to solve them? Isn't it true that the promise that was given is *more* than you need? Surely then, God will be generous with less. Ask him for the help you need in dealing with your problems *today*. There's an old Spiritual that says exactly what I mean. It goes something like this:

> *Lord don't move your mountain . . .*
> *Give me strength to climb it.*
> *You don't have to move that stumbling block,*
> *But lead me, Lord, around it.*

Give your faith a lift. *Expect* the strength and the guidance that God is going to give to you. Be ready to accept it when it comes. And only deal with one day at a time. "Therefore do not be anxious about tomorrow, for tomorrow will be anxious for itself. Let the day's own trouble be sufficient for the day" (Matthew 6:34). Try this, and you may find, to your surprise, that there are some things that can wait forever.

4. Move! Do it now. If you can, take a brisk walk. If you can't, stand up and stretch. Exercise for five minutes. Do whatever your age and physical condition let you do. If you're confined to bed or a wheelchair, you probably can still move some part of your anatomy. However you do it, get your circulation going.

Pick a chore, and do it. Finish it completely. It doesn't have to be something major. Clean the medicine chest. Sweep the front porch. Fold the laundry. Clean and organize your desk. All the time, say to yourself, "That's better!"

And it will be. You're still concerned with your problems . . . with your mountains and stumbling blocks. But you're not sitting around stewing about them. You're *doing* something about the way you look and feel, and you're getting *something,* however minor, done. You're dealing with today. A sense of accomplishment goes a long way toward banishing the blues.

April is a blessing. It's a lighthearted month, conducive to cleaning clutter from your house and mind. It's a month for renewing faith, for learning the difference between worry and concern. It's a month for banishing the blues. It's a month for believing.

Every day in the month of April, find a growing, blooming thing to look at. Study it. God made it as perfect as it is. If weeds grow around it, threatening to choke off its life, all you have to do is pull them out and throw them away. Weed the soil of your mind. Re-seed it, and feed it with faith. That's what spring housecleaning is really all about.

Thank you, Lord, for the spring of the year,
When the gardens of life are ready to bloom.
Let me search out my weeds while they are shallow-rooted.
Let me plant seeds of believing,
And feed my soul with faith,
That I may find in today
Strength to climb the mountains of my life.

5 MAY
The Touch System

We need the comrade heart
That understands,
And the warmth, the living warmth
Of human hands.
　　　　　　　　—Thomas Curtis Clark

In May the air wraps itself around us like a soft
blanket, brushes our cheeks with gentle breezes that
linger and whisper. "Feel us," they seem to say. "Look
alive, and feel us."

Our senses are forced open like the soft green buds of
flowering nectarines when they swell and open in a burst
of pink energy. We see . . . we hear . . . we smell . . . we
taste . . . but May is particularly a time for us to reach
out and touch. The world is at our fingertips. We are
touched by the vibrations of the air around us. This is the
month for reaching out and touching back.

Touching is a nourishing thing, as necessary as food.
Babies, in their instinctive wisdom, know this. They
crave closeness . . . intimacy. They cry for it. Out loud.
Pick up a sobbing baby, and watch him smile. Plant a
kiss on a childhood bump or bruise, and watch the pain
disappear.

Schoolchildren are generally touchers too. They reach
out physically, feeling people, things, and each other.
Look at them on any school ground . . . wrestling,
tickling, pushing, pulling. The proverbial pigtail in the
inkwell wasn't all naughtiness. It was just another
excuse for touching. Whatever the method, young people
manage to make contact. Holding hands is as instinctive
to them as breathing.

We adults crave contact too. But not out loud.
Somewhere along the road to maturity we begin to stand

away from each other. In shyness? In suspicion? In
loneliness? For some reason, the human hand becomes a
private thing. We guard it closely, as if we're afraid it
might become contaminated.

Haven't you seen the awkwardness when two people,
newly introduced, make halfway movements, each one
waiting for the other to hold out a hand?

I asked my son once why he hesitated. "I think Mr.
Phillips wanted to shake hands with you," I told him.
"Why didn't you just hold out your arm?"

"I was waiting for him to make the first move."

"Why?"

"Well, for Pete's sake! I would have looked pretty silly
standing there with my hand in the air. What if he didn't
want to shake it, or didn't see it or something?"

No one wants to feel rejected, or be embarrassed. So we
don't give Great Aunt Harriet a hug, because maybe she
won't respond. Or maybe we want to avoid an emotional
experience. Or maybe we don't really like her all that
much and prefer to keep our distance, doing the things
duty tells us we should do, but not touching any more
than necessary. The excuses for not touching are legion,
but unless you're avoiding a communicable disease, none
of them hold much water.

The magic of a human hand is what this chapter is all
about. It's dedicated to all of you who occasionally pull
back, like a turtle into his shell, waiting for someone else
to make the first move.

This time *you're* going to make the first move, and I'm
going to show you how. I want you to spend the first
week of May getting acquainted with your hands. Start
(right now . . . this minute) by lifting them in the air and
looking at them. Wiggle your fingers. Go on and do it.
Nobody's looking. For the rest of the week, I want you to
use your hands with a new awareness that they are
precious tools. Watch them. Look at all their parts. Notice
how efficiently they operate. Take care of them, and
make them beautiful. Don't worry about their age. Old
hands have a loveliness all their own. Only neglected
hands are unbeautiful. So give yourself a manicure once

at the beginning of the week and again on the seventh day. In between, keep those broken nails repaired and invest in a bottle of hand lotion. No one wants to be touched by hands that look and feel like they need recycling.

Three times a day, do the following exercises. (1) Open and close your fingers, making tight fists. Repeat fifty times as rapidly as possible. (2) Now hold your hands straight forward at shoulder level and, letting them go limp at the wrists, shake them as hard as you can, counting very slowly to ten. I'll bet you're aware of them now! Feel them tingle? They're alive and ready to go to work for you. (3) At least once every day, raise a hand and wave. Children are fascinated by a raised hand, held in the air and waved in greeting or farewell. Try waving at a child . . . any child . . . and see how quickly you get a response.

By the end of the seventh day, your hands will feel better than they have for years, and you'll be proud of the way they look. All this has been preparation. You've been, as it were, getting your equipment in order. Now, in the second week of May, you're ready to practice touching things.

Begin by stretching out your hand. Sophocles had something to say about that. "A prayer for peace," he said, "is an outstretched hand . . . unarmed." I think he might have added that the hand has to stretch far enough to *touch* something. So stretch out your hand, and make contact. Don't just leave it hanging there. Touch.

Spend this week feeling the world around you. Start with the sheets when you make your bed in the morning. Cool and smooth against your skin. Rub a little wet soap between your fingers and feel slippery suds. Feel the grounds when you measure out the breakfast coffee. Consider an orange! Hold it in your hand and run your fingers over its skin. Peel it. Break it open. Let the sticky juice drip over your hands. I showed an orange to a class of fifth-grade children one day and asked them to really look at it closely. There were as many reactions as there

were children in the class. "It isn't smooth after all!"
exclaimed one little girl in surprise. "And I think it has
pores in its skin, just like me."

Relish the soft silk of a rose petal, warmed by the
afternoon sun and protected by thorny branches that you
would do well to avoid. Do you have a pond near your
home? Reach down into the water and feel the cool
smoothness of the stones. Rub gently against the green
moss. Hold an ice cube in the palm of your hand for as
long as you can stand it. Place your fingers against the
pitted, rough surface of old brick. For simplicity's sake,
try a blade of grass. Gently touch the spiny edges of
holly leaves, sharp as any needle in your sewing basket.

Catch a feather in your hand and learn what gentle
really means. And now touch a dried dandelion blossom,
gray and fluffy, ready to blow. Gentleness occurs in
surprising places. Wrap your arms around the rough
trunk of a pine tree. Feel the sticky sap that oozes and
dries on the surface. All the textures and temperatures in
the world are at your fingertips. Rough, sharp, soft,
warm, cold, wet, dry . . . did you find them all?

Good! Because it's the third week of May, and you're
ready for a giant step forward. You're ready for *people*.

Now I don't mean that you should go out and begin
touching everyone in sight. I'm not talking about
grabbing either. *Touch* is the word I used. You have to be
subtle about these things. You have to use a little control.

The old rule: "Keep your hands to yourself" is not to be
discarded entirely. Because it wasn't really talking about
human contact; it was talking about invasion of privacy.
And privacy still has to be respected. The touching of
people, unlike touching things, must be done with a
certain amount of finesse. I don't want you running
around startling your friends. We are, after all, beyond
the pushing and pulling playground stage.

So here's how you go about it. Next time you're talking
to a friend, reach out casually (*casually*, I said . . . not
like a cat sneaking up on a mouse) and put a hand on
her arm. Don't make a big thing out of it, and don't hang

on. Just touch her lightly, sometime in the course of your
conversation.

That wasn't so hard, was it? You reached out, and you
didn't get burned. Your friend felt the difference, and I'll
bet you did too.

If you find that planned touching is too hard for
starters, how about practicing on that old traditional
standby, the handshake? It's something that's expected
of you from time to time, and I doubt that you'll frighten
anyone with it. It is, after all, just another way of
reaching out. Until you've mastered the handshake, you
won't get very far with the touch system anyway.

Reaching out a hand is the way strangers meet . . . and
old friends meet again. By the way, there are handshakes, and there are handshakes. Don't be a limp
fish, and don't break bones. This a friendly gesture of
good will . . . remember? Have you ever noticed that
when you shake hands with someone, you automatically
smile?

There are as many other ways of touching as there are
people to be touched. You have to use your imagination.
A little pressure on your husband's hand is as good as a
thousand words. Gentle patting soothes everything from
colic to broken hearts. And speaking of broken hearts . . .
thousands of marriages aren't what they could be,
because there isn't enough touching.

I'm not talking about sex. Making love is more than a
one-night stand. It involves a process that goes on all day
and all night and consists of things like a kiss on the
cheek, the feeling of his shoulder brushing yours, the
meeting of fingers holding the same hymnal in church,
the feel of his rough jacket wet with your tears, the
reaching out and touching under the dinner table to show
you share the same private laughter. Making love is the
joy of a caress, the warmth of a touch. How often do you
reach out to someone you love?

Take these last two weeks of May and try.

Sometimes, even when you *are* trying, you run into a
real challenge. I'm talking about the touch-me-not.

There's supposed to be one child in every family who's more independent than the rest. He doesn't want to be cuddled or patted. He's allergic to kisses and hugs. As far as mothers are concerned, he thinks they're great to have around, as long as they let him be.

That's the way it is with our middle son. By age three, he was refusing to hold hands when crossing the street. When he was seven and learned about germs, he decided that dirty hands were OK, but kisses should be examined in a biology lab. Now he's fourteen and agile.

"I can aim a kiss at his forehead," I told my husband, "and I can hear it land with a plop somewhere near the spot where he isn't anymore. For years, I've reached out to hug that boy and come up with an armful of warm air."

"Why don't you talk to him about it?" he asked.

It was worth a try. I trapped him in a doorway one day and demanded an explanation. "What's with the disappearing act? I can't seem to get my hands on you."

He grinned, "You gotta be quick!"

"What kind of answer was that?" I asked his father.

"It wasn't an answer. It was an evasion. He's embarrassed by obvious affection. He wants you to love him, but you have to be sneaky and call it something else."

I didn't know what my husband was talking about until one day when I walked into the kitchen and found the table already set for supper.

"Well, bless your heart!" I said to our daughter. She glanced up from her book and gave me a blank look. Then a voice from the living room said, "I did it."

I went in and surveyed my son, the touch-me-not. He turned scarlet. "Just don't kiss me," he begged.

"How about a hug?"

"That neither, but you could rub my back . . ."

There's one in every family. Independent, a noncuddler, allergic to kisses, a real touch-me-not. That's what he'd *like* you to believe. As for me, I'm becoming a pretty good back-rubber. My son doesn't say

much about it, but if I listen closely, I can almost hear
him purring.

The point is that your touch can be affectionate and
full of love without being obvious. Even to a touch-me-
not.

It's the end of the month and time to take stock. Look
back over the last thirty-one days and see what you've
accomplished. Remember that your hands are precious
assets. Continue taking care of them. Use them. Reach
out with them, and feel the world around you. Reach out
with them and touch your fellowman.

Jesus was a toucher, probably the greatest toucher of
all. He pulled back his hand from no man. And his
instructions, passed down to the rest of us, are clear.
You'll find them in Matthew 25:40. "Truly, I say to you,
as you did it to one of the least of these my brethren, you
did it to me."

Whether you reach out in comfort, in joy, in love, or
simply, as Socrates said, "with an outstretched hand . . .
unarmed," God is closer than you think. He is at your
fingertips.

Thank you, Lord, for the gift of my hands,
For the ability to feel.
Make me unafraid to reach out . . .
And make me always willing
To accept the offer of an outstretched hand.

6 JUNE
Come On In . . .
The Water's Fine

For yesterday is but a dream,
And tomorrow is only a vision;
But today well lived
Makes every yesterday a dream of happiness,
And every tomorrow a vision of hope.
Look well, therefore, to this day!
—author unknown

I always think of June as the month that sits in the center of the year. It's midway between seasons. It's the hub of time, around which the year turns.

June always seemed like the "now" month of our childhoods. It signified the end of school and the beginning of summer freedom. All children look forward to June with anticipation. It was the time when good things were bound to start happening. When it was over, we looked back with nostalgia. It was time to move on into the heat of summer. But June had been the magic time, the center of the year, with the past on one side and the future on the other. Do you remember how it was?

June is still a magic month. Being in it is a little like standing on top of a mountain. From June, you can see in all directions: backwards to yesterday, forward to tomorrow, and right now . . . today.

What does this have to do with becoming the whole person God wants you to be? A lot, because there are three time zones in all our lives. Yesterday . . . today . . . tomorrow. And there is a unity in past, present, and future that needs to be understood. The past is not lost to us; memory preserves it. The future is not out of reach; it's just around the corner. And the present? Well, you'd

better fall in love with today, because it's what you have.
This minute . . . now.

June is our vantage point. The place from which we
can take time by the tail and look at each of the three
zones. First, let's take a look at what's already happened.
I think more advice has been given about what to do
with the past than with any other area of time. More
often than not, we are told to "forget it." It was Ralph
Waldo Emerson who told us to "Finish each day and be
done with it. . . . You have done what you could . . ." In
other words, don't live in the past. It's foolish to cry over
spilt milk. By the same token, if you accomplished
something great in a given day, hurrah for you. But don't
spend all your tomorrows basking in past glory.

Advice like that is meant to keep people like you and
me from dwelling on what happened yesterday, from
literally moving in and living there. But . . . hear this . . .
it doesn't mean that we can't visit.

Go right ahead and indulge in a little nostalgia.
Remembering can be a good thing. There's nothing
wrong with stepping into the past as long as you don't
stay too long. After all, some of the world's best-loved
stories came right out of somebody's memories. What fun
we would have missed if Samuel Clemens and Laura
Ingalls Wilder had refused to look back.

So take time every day for remembering. Organize your
thoughts so that your mind does more than wander. Do it
like this:

1. Think of some *event* from your past.
2. Think of some *one* from your past.
3. Learn a lesson. It's true that what has been . . . has
been. But even if you can't go back and do it over, you
can learn something from it. Experience is worth a lot, so
feel a little gratitude for your mistakes. While you're at it,
find a little tolerance for yourself.
4. Take comfort. Remembrance can be healing. Have
you ever noticed how we tend to remember only the best
of things past? The bad parts fade until they're not so
painful. The good old days may not have been all that
good, but when they're seen through the tinted glasses of

memory, they look a lot rosier. Life's awful moments can
finally produce a smile. Better yet, today's problems
shrink to their proper sizes when we look at them in
perspective. We know from experience that what seems
awful this morning won't be so bad ten years from now.
What is pretty good today will be even better when we
look back on it. Enjoy looking back, even if it's only
because you're glad you're not there now.

5. Smile. Where's your sense of humor? Laugh at the
little things . . . the foolish things. Refuse to burden
yourself with regrets. Try to recapture the joys you felt as
a child. Let them live in you again. Listen to these words
of wisdom, written by a man with no regrets:

> *Who may regret what was, since it has made*
> *Himself himself? All that I was I am,*
> *And the old childish joy now lives in me*
> *At sight of a green field or a green tree.*
> —John Freeman

Where are *your* childish joys? Spend a little time each day
seeing if you can bring them to the surface and feel them
again.

6. Remember that you're only visiting. Don't stay in
the past too long. There is a great deal of difference
between walking in the mainstream of life and standing
still in a puddle. Take time for remembering, but don't get
stagnant. A few minutes a day are enough.

Now it's time to take a deep breath and dive right
into today. It's the "now" time of your life. It's "where
it's at!" Just watch out that you don't start panting and
hyperventilating. That's where you get into trouble with
today. You try too hard to do too much too soon,
forgetting that one step . . . one breath at a time . . .
is the way to go.

When you wake up in the morning, you don't face a
year or a month or a week. You're looking at that single,
beautiful minute of aliveness called *now*. Get up a little
early some morning and listen to the sounds of today. A

leaf falling. A bird scolding. Somebody's alarm clock. The wind in the trees. A car chugging by. Don't think. Don't criticize. Just listen. It's all part of your world. Be glad you're facing the time of your life. You can do anything you want with it. Jump right into the mainstream. Don't waste a moment standing in a puddle!

Is jumping hard for you? Do you have a problem making decisions? Do you wonder which way to go now? One afternoon I overheard a young mother talking to her daughter at a busy intersection. She was obviously teaching the child about the whys and wherefores of traffic lights.

"Now watch, Beth, and see how the colors change," she instructed. The crowd was large and the traffic heavy. Beth was confused.

"Which way do I go?" she demanded.

"Take your time," her mother said. "Watch for the green light. Look both ways before you make up your mind. But when you do decide, don't just stand there. *Move!*"

When the light finally changed, Beth reminded me of the small boy getting ready to jump off the high dive for the first time. He stood there balancing for quite awhile. But when he finally made up his mind to dive, he took a deep breath, squared his shoulders, and *moved!*

When you jump off the high dive into life, you don't just skim the surface. You plunge deep and come up again for a breath of air. This doesn't mean that you're always going to find yourself in fresh, clear, spring water. Some days you'll even feel like you're knee-deep in mud. *Unless:* you learn the secret approach to any situation. It's simply "getting psyched up." Believe it or not, we human beings can talk ourselves into almost any state of mind. And what's the matter with that, as long as the state of mind is positive.

Don't be like my friend Susan . . . who goes through life with a built-in negative attitude. Failure, she testifies, is just around the corner. If she bakes a cake, it's liable to fall. The dress she's sewing probably won't fit. The people who are invited to dinner at her house either **won't come,** or if they do, they won't like what's on the table.

"Susan," I asked her, "why do you go around **expecting** trouble?"

"It's safer that way," she said. "It's better **to expect** the worst. Then, when it happens, you won't **be dis-** appointed."

Susan was defeated before she started. She **reminded** me of an old-time comic strip called "Sad Sack," **whose** main character went through life courting **disaster. He** expected it, and it obliged him by coming his **way.**

What Susan didn't realize was that she was **psyching** herself up for trouble. "Oh, well . . . what can **you** expect?" became her byword. "I might have **known** things would turn out this way," became her motto. **"Just** my luck!" became her battle cry.

Today, for Susan, is not a blessing. It's something **she** has to survive. Last time I talked to her, she **was** a discontented, peevish woman, who wondered **aloud why** life had to dish out so many problems and hand **them to** her. The past was the only place where Susan **found** any comfort. She shook her head at today, **and hid her** eyes from tomorrow.

That's not jumping off the high dive. It's **standing in a** stagnant puddle of discontent.

People deal with today in surprising ways. Take, **for** example, Harriet Appleby, a charming older **lady who** loves to have visitors and is not, by any **stretch of the** imagination, discontented. I stopped by her **house one** day to say hello. She was deeply engrossed **in reading** of the latest romantic novels. A little reluctantly, **I** thought, she laid it down carefully beside her.

"This is the eighth book I've read this week," **she** confided. "I don't know what I'll do if my eyesight **goes,** because reading is so important to me. It helps **to pass** the time."

Harriet had taken up residence in a dream **world. She** was glad when friends came to see her, but she **was even** happier when they got up to leave. She was **more excited** about the characters in her books than she was about the people in her living room.

Reading is important to me, too, and don't think for a minute that I'm knocking the value and pleasure of books. After all, I'm writing one. But when your major occupation and interest achieves nothing more than passed time, you need a new set of values.

Harriet's attitude isn't negative. She's as cheery as can be. But she has compromised with living and settled for waiting. I couldn't help being reminded of the story of the prisoner who marked off his days in long notches on the stone wall. It got to be such an absorbing task that he stopped trying to escape. When someone finally freed him, he sighed as he went out the door and was heard muttering, "Two more notches, and I would have had one hundred."

So what should *your* attitude toward today be? No matter what your age, you can take a tip from Stuart Carter, who remains busy and active, even in his eighties. When asked how he managed to live such an active life at his age, he replied, with a twinkle in his eye, "I'll tell you my secret. I get the newspaper every morning, and turn to the obituaries. If I don't see my name anywhere, I say to myself, 'Stuart, you're not dead yet.' And then I get busy living!"

Stuart, unlike Susan and Harriet, is psyched up to live. I really don't think he has time for the obituaries, because he is too busy living twenty-four hours a day. Whatever his age, he's made up his mind that he's not dead yet, and he's not going to spend his time sitting around waiting for trouble. The best years of Stuart's life are not "back then" or "someday." Today, for Stuart, is forever, and he is forever young.

I'm not telling you that you have to check the papers every morning, but you *can* take a tip from a wise man. No matter what your age, you're not dead yet . . . unless you choose to act that way. Every single morning, say to yourself, "*This* is the time of my life."

This minute . . . right now . . . is the point of time you

are in. It's yesterday's future, and it's soon to be tomorrow!

What *about* tomorrow? The Dominican Sisters of Bethany, Boston, have a motto, which goes like this: "God does not care what you've been, only what you are." We might expand that to include . . . "He also cares about what you're going to *become*." For you *are* going to become *something*, whether you like it or not.

A few years ago we all went around singing, "*Que será . . . será*. Whatever will be . . . will be." Don't you believe it! Whatever will be is a consequence of a number of things, and fate isn't one of them. Your world, you know, is just as big as you let it be. So is your future.

I saw a sign on a little church in the desert. In big, bold letters it commanded, "If you must throw cold water on things, be a fireman." When you sit back with a sigh and a look of resignation and say, "Whatever will be . . . will be," you're tossing ice water on your own potential. Whatever will be has a lot to do with you. *You* can set the pace for your tomorrows by what you do today. Here's how:

1. Look forward to tomorrow. It always comes. So you might as well step right up and get your ticket. Stop being afraid of what might be waiting around the next corner, because nothing's there until you get there. Look forward to the future: it's everybody's second chance.

2. Every single day, take time to dream. A little wishful thinking never hurt anyone. There's nothing wrong with occasionally having your head in the clouds. It's when you bury it in the sand like an ostrich that you get into trouble. So lift up your eyes and look beyond the tip of your nose. Reach for the stars. Wish on one. Your dreams may not all come true, but you're taking a step in the right direction. Anyway, wishing on a star isn't superstitious. It's just a way of stopping for a moment and putting into words the way you would like things to be.

While you're at it, be a definite dreamer. Not like my young friend, Cynthia. It was an afternoon in June when she closed her book with a snap and gazed longingly out her bedroom window. Two more weeks, and school would be out. Right now, life was a drag. But things would soon be different. Summer was coming, and she intended to have the time of her life. She didn't have any definite plans. She just knew that things would be better later. She would start enjoying life as soon as the last bell rang.

This isn't dreaming. It's discontent. When you dream, be specific. Don't waste all that precious energy on vague unhappiness. "All things are possible to him who believes" (Mark 9:23). So get in there and dream about something you can believe in.

Time is something you spend, whether you like it or not. You can get a good or bad bargain. It's up to you. Waste it, and you get nothing in return. Cram it too full, and you overload your circuits. Measure it out carefully . . . spend it wisely . . . and you'll have the time of your life . . . today *and* tomorrow.

Take the magic month of June to recognize the three time zones. Pay your regards to yesterday, and look forward to tomorrow. But remember to spend your time wisely in today. It's all yours. Decide to become a gambler. Take a chance on life. It's one game you can win. As a friend said to me on the eve of my fortieth birthday, "Come on in. The water's fine!"

Help me, Lord, to spend wisely
Your gift of days.
Show me how to learn from the past,
and plant seeds of future hope.
Teach me especially
To treasure life's precious moments,
Placing my todays
In your guiding hands.

7 JULY
Know the Word

Man shall not live by bread alone,
but by every word that proceeds from the
*   mouth of God.*
                              —Matthew 4:4

If of thy mortal goods thou art bereft,
And from thy slender store two loaves are left,
Sell, sell thou one, and with the dole,
Buy hyacinths . . . to feed thy soul.
                              —Mushariff-ud-din (Sa'di)

Every now and then we all need the pause that refreshes. Even more than the pause, we need the refreshment. I'm not talking about ice cold cola. I'm talking about those things that keep us from going stale, that give us new life, that inspire, lifting the tiredness from our bodies and minds. In short, I'm talking about "hyacinths": those beautiful things and thoughts that remind us that we humans do not live by bread alone.

What better time than the month of July to reach out for something refreshing? July, when the sun beats down relentlessly, when the days are long, and we yearn for a quiet spot in the shade. July, when our physical comfort is so demanding, has to be the ideal time to remind ourselves that our spirits also are in need of refreshing.

It's true. Man really doesn't live by bread alone. It may be the staff of life, but you and I have to have something more. Never, never will you put together all your missing parts until you add some inspiration, some beauty, to your daily living.

How do you go about finding this spiritual soul food that's missing in your life? Where do you look for guidance?

The Puritans had an old saying that puts us on the right track. Good nourishment, they said, is brown bread . . . as well as the gospel. Practical people, those Puritans. They knew the necessity of daily bread. Right along with it, they recognized the need for another kind of sustenance. And they knew where to look for it.

You can find it too. This may come as a shocker, but the easiest way is to open your Bible. In these days of mass produced literature and instant entertainment, the Bible, believe it or not, is still good reading. All the answers are right there, under one cover, waiting for you to find them. It has all the inspiration you need to brighten your day, all the beauty and poetry you need to feed your soul. The Bible is a book full of hyacinths. You only have to look.

When I was a child, we played a little game. It involved closing the Bible, then opening it again at random, running an index finger down the pages, and searching for a verse meant for you alone. Whatever the problem, whatever the need, whatever your heart was full of, a verse was always there, somewhere, that seemed to fit perfectly.

Try it for yourself. Pick up your Bible for five minutes every day. If you don't find the inspiration you need the first time you open the book, turn the pages. Now listen! I'm not trying to tell you that you're handling some sort of magical book of tricks. What I'm saying is that the Bible is so chock-full of words of wisdom and guidance that every page has something to offer. You're just liable to open the book and find what you need right there staring you in the face. If you don't, don't go all to pieces and slam it shut. God gave you two strong hands and ten fingers. Use them. Turn those pages until you *do* find what you need. I promise that you won't be disappointed . . . and you won't have to turn too many pages either.

Do you doubt me? I expected that you might. That's why I decided recently to keep a one-month record of my own daily reading. I bought a small spiral notebook and wrote a date at the top of each page, beginning with the

first day of the month. Beneath that, I made a short
reference to whatever was bothering me that morning. If
I had some particular problem or worry, I gave it a name.
If everything looked rosy, I described those feelings too.
You don't always have to have problems, you know.
Some days are made for rejoicing!

Each day I opened the Bible and began looking,
running my index finger down the page, sometimes
stopping and sometimes moving right along. It wasn't
long before I found what I was looking for. Verses that
seemed meant just for me at that particular morning in
my life. It never failed. Sometimes I found them
immediately. Sometimes I had to look awhile. But as
soon as I did find them, I copied them and their
references into my notebook.

I was working regularly as a substitute teacher, when
what seemed like a golden-opportunity full-time job came
along. It would mean long hours, but it intrigued me.
Trying to make a decision was agonizing. My loyalties
were divided. We still had teen-age children. The new
hours would mean that I would see them on the run. I
was writing daily and selling steadily in the free-lance
market. The new job would mean that any writing was
relegated to late evenings. I valued that time with my
husband. How much was I going to sacrifice? I'll admit
that the extra money seemed substantial. The prestige
was ego-raising. But still I hesitated. It got to the point
where I had to make a decision.

One morning I picked up my Bible and turned to 2
Kings 14:10. "Be content with your glory, and stay at
home . . ." it said. I laughed aloud. But I thought about it.
Only a few days later I found out what that golden-
opportunity job would have been like. "Disastrous," said
the woman who took it. It was the worst decision she had
ever made.

Soon after, I began writing this book. It was a
challenge, and I had some doubts. Who was I, after all, to
tell other people what to do? Could I count on God to give
me the guidance I needed? Here's what I found on the

first try. "Then the Lord said to me, 'Take a large tablet and write upon it in common characters . . .' " (Isaiah 8:1). I couldn't believe it. I felt as if I'd received a gentle prod in the right direction. Shaking my head, I flipped back a few pages and saw what everyone should read when about to take on a new responsibility. "Cast your bread upon the waters, for you will find it after many days" (Ecclesiastes 11:1). It was all the encouragement I wanted.

One day I took my morning coffee out to the patio and opened my eyes to an exceptional day. The sky was blue, the clouds fluffy white; the orioles made yellow patches among green leaves, and the air was strong with the fragrance of dew-tipped roses. It was so beautiful I could almost taste it. The author of Psalm 34 must have felt the same way. There were his words bouncing back at me from the page: "O taste and see that the Lord is good!" Yet again I read,

> *for lo, the winter is past,*
> *the rain is over and gone.*
> *The flowers appear on the earth,*
> *the time of singing has come,*
> *and the voice of the turtledove*
> *is heard in our land*
> (Song of Solomon 2:11, 12).

Sometimes reading beautiful words that accurately describe your feelings is all that you need to start you out in the right direction. Sometimes all you need from the Scriptures are beautiful words to lift your spirit. "The wind blows where it wills, and you hear the sound of it, but you do not know whence it comes or whither it goes . . ." (John 3:8). "Let us go out early to the vineyards and see whether the vines have budded, whether the grape blossoms have opened and the pomegranates are in bloom" (Song of Solomon 7:12). It's true that "times of refreshing may come from the presence of the Lord" (Acts 3:19).

My Bible falls open easily to Joshua 1:9, because I've
had to return to these words so many times. "Be strong
and of good courage; be not frightened, neither be
dismayed; for the Lord your God is with you wherever you
go." Not one of us can deny fear. If you haven't felt it,
you haven't been around much. Whether it's a trip to the
dentist or the welfare of your children that's bothering
you, a word of comfort and assurance is in order. If you
want specifics, try turning to the story of the young
David and have a look at his attitude when he had to
face *his* Goliath. You'll find it in 1 Samuel 17:31-49.

Then there are those times when, no matter how dense
the crowd around you, you feel alone. Read Psalm 71,
verse 3. " . . . thou art my rock and my fortress." I found
it one morning when I needed it, and then I remembered
some other verses and searched until I found them. They
are at the very end of the book of Matthew. " . . . lo, I am
with you alway, even unto the end of the world"
(Matthew 28:20, King James Version). Can you read
those words and feel that you are alone? Hardly!

All of us who have children have had moments of
discouragement. Are they listening? Are they learning?
One morning when I was really wondering if I was doing
all the right things, I ran my index finger down the page
and read: "Train up a child in the way he should go, and
when he is old he will not depart from it" (Proverbs 22:6).
It was just the encouragement I needed. Especially when
I was reminded that we parents aren't really working
alone. God is doing his part when he promises to " . . .
take a sprig from the lofty top of the cedar . . . break off
from the topmost of its young twigs a tender one, and . . .
plant it upon a high and lofty mountain . . . that it may
bring forth boughs and bear fruit, and become a noble
cedar . . ." (Ezekiel 17:22, 23).

Speaking of children, do you ever feel that you're
everybody's servant? Do you cook and clean and mend
and tend, then do it all over again? Of course you do. On
the days when all this drudgery begins to get you down,
turn, as I did, to Luke and read (22: 27): "For which is the

greater, one who sits at table, or one who serves? Is it not the one who sits at table? But I am among you as one who serves." I'll never forget how good these words made me feel. I was no longer "put upon." Serving does not have to be slavery. There's an important difference.

One day I got up on the wrong side of the bed. It happens to the best of us. After stumbling and grumbling my way through sack lunches and spilled milk, I came across these lines:

> *It is better to live in a corner of the*
> *housetop*
> *than in a house shared with a*
> *contentious woman* (Proverbs 21:9).

That one slowed me down and took the scowl off my face. I had to stop and laugh, for God had been one step ahead of me again.

How do you deal with vicious gossip? How do you handle the temptation to pass on an unverified story? It's a common problem, and you have to learn the difference between talking *about* people, which is a normal part of conversation, and putting people *down*, which is not. Turn to Psalm 101 and read verse 2. I found it one morning and have turned back to it often.

> *I will walk with integrity of heart*
> *within my house;*
> *I will not set before my eyes anything that is base.*

We all like to get credit for what we do; it's a good feeling to have someone else appreciate your efforts. Believe it or not, it's an even better feeling to give quietly, even secretly. I remember when I was a child and May Day did not mean a distress signal. It was a special day. We decorated little baskets to fill with flowers and place on a neighbor's doorstep . . . in secret. It was a beautiful custom and could stand a rebirth, for it taught children

something vital: the thrill of giving pleasure without
reward.

Oh, but there *was* reward! The very best kind. I
remember how we put the flowers carefully on the step
and rang the doorbell. Then we ran and hid, because it
was essential that the gift remain a secret one. The
reward was the expression on someone's face when the
door opened, and the May basket was revealed. I
remember how one elderly lady picked up the flowers and
buried her face in them. Then she looked searchingly
around the yard. I held my breath and waited until she
closed the door. It was a precious thing, my secret, and I
kept very still, because the magic would evaporate if I
told my name. I had given "hyacinths," you see. And I
had received more in my silence than I had given. (So
had my friends. For lack of solving the mystery, our
elderly lady looked upon *all* of us with special kindness!)

What does this May basket story have to do with Bible
verses? Plenty, because sometimes we need a gentle
reminder of things we have stored away in the backs of
our minds. I opened my Bible one morning and turned to
Matthew. The word "secret" came leaping out of the
page, and I read from the sixth chapter, verses 3, 4:
" . . . when you give alms, do not let your left hand know
what your right hand is doing, so that your alms may be
in secret; and your Father who sees in secret will reward
you." I had forgotten that secret giving is something
special. I knew it as a child, but as a woman I needed
reminding that hyacinths are bought with love.

Now then, are you a worrier? Are you anxious about
tomorrow . . . and the day after that? Start your day with
the book of Matthew and remind yourself to take life one
step at a time. Read Matthew 6:25-34. It's a long passage,
but well worth reading. My Bible fell open to it one day
when I felt that things were piling up on me, and my
appointment calendar didn't have any white squares left.
It gave me the comforting pat on the back I needed, the
assurance that everything would work out, and the
reminder that anxiety gets you nowhere. " . . . do not be

anxious about tomorrow, for tomorrow will be anxious for
itself. Let the day's own trouble be sufficient for the day"
(Matthew 6:34).

After a day of teaching a particularly difficult class of
eighth graders, nearly all with behavior problems, many
with worse problems, I came home full of anything but
brotherly love. These verses, quickly found, made it
possible for me to go back and try again: " . . . for he
makes his sun rise on the evil and on the good, and
sends rain on the just and on the unjust" (Matthew 5:45).
"Truly, I say to you, as you did it to one of the least of
these my brethren, you did it to me" (Matthew 25:40).
"There are varieties of gifts, but the same Spirit; and
there are varieties of service, but the same Lord; and
there are varieties of working, but it is the same God who
inspires them all in every one" (1 Corinthians 12:4-6). It
takes all kinds, I thought to myself, and God is just as
interested in these problem children as he is in me.

Keep your own diary. Get a small notebook and take a
page for each day. Jot down the date and a few words
describing any problems that faced you that morning, or
just the way you felt. Below that, identify the Bible verses
that you found helpful, and write at least a few key
words from the verses. By the end of a month you should
be well on your way to having a guidebook for your own
personal devotions, reflecting your own private needs.

I should give you fair warning. The beauty and power
of the words you read are not to be reckoned with. You're
liable to be swept along for more than your daily five
minutes. You *might* even decide to read the whole book.
Why not? Nobody says you have to do it in any special
order. There are no rules, as far as I know. I do know
that reading the Bible is like opening up a fresh box of
chocolates. Once you get started, it's hard to stop.

Don't be afraid to read different translations.
Sometimes new wording gives fresh insight. And don't
get uptight over what you don't understand. I don't
understand calculus or trigonometry, but I don't let that
stop me from balancing my checkbook. Anyway, Mark
Twain once said that what he didn't understand in the

Bible didn't bother him at all. What got under his skin was what he *did* understand.

Don't be afraid to read between the lines. The spirit of God is there, too. Let's face it: the Bible doesn't tell all the details. People in those days got up in the mornings and washed their faces. Prophets got headaches, just like the rest of us. Women occasionally burned their dinners, and they always had to wash the clothes. People laughed, and people cried. Children played in the sun and rain. Use your imagination. Don't be uncomfortable with the Bible.

Even if, at first, you feel a little like the small boy in church who confided to his mother, "I tried to just sit there and cross my eyes and pretend I was somewhere else, but it didn't work. The minister's voice kept coming through" . . . relax. With a little practice, you'll learn to let God's voice through without a struggle.

One day I was reading in the Gospel of John and was suddenly aware that I was getting something extra. I was reading in complete scenes and pictures instead of just black words on a white page. I was *there*, in between the lines, watching and listening. Remember the old hymn, "Were You There?" You *can* be there! It's as simple as using your two hands to open a book. Use your imagination and read the Word. It's the most exciting story in the world. Through it you can follow Abraham across the desert. You can watch David face his Goliath and see Egypt through Joseph's eyes. Most important, you can join Jesus in the world of two thousand years ago. You can hear the message loud and clear.

By the way, how do you *feel* about the book itself, now that you've got it in your hands? Do you hold it carefully, so it will stay shiny and new? If you feel like you're in a classroom with the teacher looking over your shoulder, you've got the wrong idea. The Bible is there for you to *use*. Don't be afraid to pick up a pencil and draw a line under something you want to remember. As a matter of fact, it's not a bad idea to draw a line under *all* the helpful verses you find. They will be easier to find when you look for them again.

I'm always a little skeptical of the large, unused Bible that sits in a place of honor in the living room, especially if it's covered with a layer of dust. A minister friend of mine is fond of telling what he calls his favorite Bible story. It seems that he went to call on two elderly ladies who lived in his parish. They were sisters and had shared the same home for years. While the three of them sat, having tea, there arose a difference of opinion on a biblical question. Sara, sure that she was in the right, and determined to prove it, opened the large, ornate Bible that sat on the coffee table. The huge book made noisy, popping sounds as its hinges strained, and the crisp, unused pages crackled as Sara separated them carefully.

Mattie was sitting all this time in her chair, impatiently crossing one leg and then the other. Finally, when she couldn't stand it any longer, she jumped up and rushed out of the room. The next ten minutes were filled with the sounds of cupboards slamming all over the house. Reverend Whitfield claims that he even heard the distinct click of the refrigerator door, opening and shutting.

Sara continued turning stiff pages, each time fanning a little more dust around the surface of the coffee table. At last, Mattie returned, clutching a well-worn Bible, its black front covered with flour.

"You'll never dream where I found it," she laughed.

Reverend Whitfield admits that he thought she would never find anything at all. But he had misjudged Mattie. It wasn't until she reappeared, brushing flour from the book's surface, that he realized what had been happening. She was hunting for that Bible in much the same way he had hunted for his glasses that very morning.

"I just had them a second ago," he'd said to his wife.

Most of us treat our car keys the same way. We use them so much that we tend to set them down unthinkingly and forget where we put them.

When Mattie flipped open the pages and handed the book to him, he saw that some areas were heavily

underlined. Sometimes there were even notes written in
the margins.

"Hmph!" snorted Sara. "Some people never learn how
to take care of their Bibles!" She kept right on turning
her crisp pages. But it didn't matter anymore. Mattie had
already found the answer in her well-floured Scriptures.

Now, I'm not telling you to cook with your Bible in one
hand, and I'm not advising you to treat the Bible with
anything but reverence. The point is this: letting it gather
dust in one spot is *not* reverence. It's not even reading.
Better to wear it out reading it, than never to open it at all.

Now that you understand the importance of reading
the Word, I have something startling to tell you. The
Bible isn't a stopping place. The Word of God is an
ongoing thing, not confined between the covers of a book.
That's right. To know the Word, you have to do more
than read it. You have to be aware of it in a hundred
different ways.

Martin Luther said it well. "God writes the gospel not
in the Bible alone, but on the trees, and flowers, and
clouds and stars."

Look around you and listen. The word of God is being
written every day. God's signature traces the rainbow
and follows the wind. His voice reaches us in the sounds
of music, and in that still, small feeling that tells us we're
not alone. He speaks to us through other men, who reach
out, sometimes gropingly, in art and poetry and science,
and lift their faces to the stars.

What is it, then, that you should do, knowing that
bread is not enough, and that the need for hyacinths is
basic to every human soul?

You should take time in the month of July to read the
word of God in a ray of sunshine, warm and bright. See
it in summer raindrops, trickling down a pane of glass.
Feel it in green leaves, crisp and cool. Look up and watch
for it in the stars. Listen for it. Search it out. Each time
you find it, write it permanently on your heart.

Know it well, and you will have more than bread. You
will have an armful of hyacinths to feed your soul.

Thank you, Lord, for the beauty
Of the Word
That you offer freely,
As a gift of love.
Help me to reach out
With open arms
And embrace those things
That feed the soul.

8 AUGUST
Close Your Eyes
So You Can See

That inward eye
Which is the bliss of solitude.
        —William Wordsworth

August is the hottest month, at least in our part of the country. When I was a child, it was also the slowest month. Schoolbooks were tossed aside, and there were days of lazy glory spent dreaming. Air-conditioning, in those days, consisted of an electric fan which rotated, hopefully, sending a rush of cooling air against your skin. Then you had to sit still and wait, hot and sticky, until it came back and pointed at you again. It was hot in August inside and outside; we slowed down out of necessity in the middle of the day. The evenings were long, and filled with children's shouts and the smell of watermelon. But August mornings were special. They still are.

The world comes alive earlier on a morning in August than in any other month of the year. I think the bees must get started before the sun comes up. When it's still barely light, the morning air loses its chill and hangs warmly over the garden. It's a wonderful time to be out of doors.

Now wait a minute! Before you yawn and pull the covers over your head, hear me out. You may hate to get up early in the morning, but don't close the book yet. I'm going to show you how to get a head start on the day and improve your eyesight at the same time. Let me tell you a story.

It was on an August morning, years ago, that I learned to close my eyes and improve my sight. I was being punished. My sister and I had committed some now-forgotten crime, and our mother, in exasperation, had sent us in disgrace to the backyard. Our punishment was "nothing." That's what we were told to do. Nothing. We weren't even allowed to speak to each other or to anyone else.

"Just sit there and twiddle your thumbs," Mother ordered. "And if you get tired of that, close your eyes, and listen to the grass grow."

Ridiculous? That's what we thought. But we tried it out of boredom. The result was a shocker. Because we found out that with our eyes closed, all our other senses came alive. We never really heard the grass grow, but we listened to a whole new world around us. We heard vital things, like a busy mockingbird snapping off a twig way up in the top of the Chinese elm . . . like thousands of leaves beating a hushed rhythm in the hot air. Our children's minds stopped churning for a few precious moments. While the green grass grew, the kaleidoscope slowed, and, with our eyes closed, we saw the world in focus.

We did this naturally, unaffectedly, as children, without worrying about how or why it was happening. We accepted the results just as naively. Small miracles are, after all, perfectly normal when you're a child. We played the game often, delighting in the new sensations and laughing with pleasure at how bright and new the world always seemed when we opened our eyes again.

Somehow, along the way to adulthood, I became too busy for quiet, unproductive moments like those. It wasn't until I was in my thirties with a big family and an equally big old house to take care of, that I discovered that listening to the sounds of growing grass is more than a juvenile game.

Once again, it was a morning in August. This time my feet hurt! I was up before anyone else, frying chicken for a picnic later in the day. I'd cleaned house the day before, and I was tired. Bone weary. The sun came up and cast golden rays through the kitchen window. All I remember thinking was that it was a terrible time to be up in the morning.

I could hear the rest of the family stirring around in the bedrooms upstairs. They shouldn't complain, I thought. They were just beginning to stretch in their warm beds, while I had been slaving in the kitchen for over an hour. I put a bowl of milk down for the cat and opened a can of food for our dog, who licked at my hand affectionately.

"*You* don't have to cook chicken for an army," I told him. I was the world's A-1 martyr, and I wasn't being a good sport about it.

What was the matter with me? I'd better do something to brighten my mood, or I was going to ruin the day for everyone. After all, it had been my idea to get an early start. I just hadn't realized how things were going to pile up that week.

I took my coffee out into the backyard and sat down in a patio chair. Wordsworth had been right, I thought, and I found myself remembering the poet's words and repeating them aloud.

> *The world is too much with us: late and soon,*
> *Getting and spending, we lay waste our powers:*
> *Little we see in Nature that is ours . . .*

"We are out of tune," he goes on to say. And indeed I was.

"O Lord," I muttered, "I'm tired, and discouraged, and I wish I didn't feel this way." I felt like just sitting there and closing my eyes against the intrusion of the disorder I found around me. Why not? I did close them . . . and found myself remembering back to another time. I hadn't expected to hear the grass grow then, and I didn't expect to hear it now. But I was surprised at what did happen. The old magic wasn't gone, but this time it was more than a childhood game.

With my eyes closed, my other senses took over. The warm air was suddenly alive with sound. I recognized the heavy, tireless droning of bees. They sounded like armies,

hovering over the roses. What was that soft sighing that
rose and fell like music from an unseen woodwind? I
tipped my head and listened. It came from the northern
corner of our lot, where the land rises into a little hill
beyond the kitchen. My husband and I had planted seven
small pine trees there fifteen years before. I was
ashamed. I should have recognized the sound of the
breeze moving through their branches. I was, I told
myself, forgetting how to listen.

And listening wasn't all. I felt the sun-warmed air on
my skin, brushing gently across my cheek, and carrying
with it the fragrance of hot-weather roses, sultry and
sweet. How could I have missed these things? How,
indeed, could I have been so blind? I ran my fingers over
the rough redwood of the chair arm, then bent to feel the
brick patio floor. The sun was warming it already. I was
warm, but with a glow that had nothing to do with the
sun. For, as I straightened up and opened my eyes, the
miracle happened. My backyard had never looked like
this before. Everything was in place; nothing had been
moved about. That's not what I mean. The change was
in color and focus. The tree leaves sparkled. Surely they
hadn't been that green all the time! And they were so
clear, each one standing out in detail. Above my head the
sky was blue . . . really blue . . . with a single white cloud
that curled at the corners. Unripe pomegranates swayed
gently, still pink, and the lemon tree in the corner
boasted three yellow fruit.

For one precious moment I could see clearly . . . more
clearly than ever before, because I was still aware of my
other senses, all working together. I heard, smelled, felt,
looked, yes . . . even tasted of the miracle of everyday things.

When finally, reluctantly, I took my coffee back to the
house, I could meet my family with a smile. A day that
starts with a miracle can't be all bad.

What's that? You could use the time in better ways?
There are a hundred extra things you need to get done?
You just don't go in for that kind of self-indulgence? You
must have been reading Ecclesiastes (11:4).

He who observes the wind will not sow;
And he who regards the clouds will not reap.

It's a good lesson. I have no argument with it. He who gets down to business gets things done. We all know that. But we should also listen well to what Jesus had to say to the apostles when they were busy getting things done. They returned to Jesus, and told him all that they had done and taught. There was much more to be done, and time was growing short. Did Jesus send them right back to finish their work? No. He said instead, "Come away by yourselves to a lonely place, and rest a while" (Mark 6:30, 31).

Jesus knew the value of a five-minute break. I imagine that he often shut his eyes and felt the sun-warmed air on his face. It was Jesus who said, "Your eye is the lamp of your body; when your eye is sound, your whole body is full of light . . ." (Luke 11:34). This says a good deal about the value of seeing clearly. If you're out of focus, you need to close those eyes and refuel the lamps. It's almost the same thing as putting in the plug to recharge a drained battery. Here's how to start:

1. Get out of bed. Go outside. Find the quietest place in your garden. You don't have a garden? No matter. Maybe you have a porch, or a balcony. If you can't go outside, sit by a window. If you can't do this exercise until later in the day, and your only chance is your lunch hour, head for the park downtown.

2. Find a seat. Any old chair will do. A bench. A kitchen stool. A large rock. Don't waste time, and don't make excuses. Lacking all else, throw a towel on the grass and sit on it.

3. Close your eyes. Relax your eyelids until they stop fluttering. Don't open them again, no matter what, for five minutes. You don't need a timer. If done correctly, these exercises will take no more than five minutes.

4. Become aware of the darkness. That's all there is for you to see . . . just the darkness at the back of your eyelids. For the next few minutes, you're not going to be distracted by lights or colors or shapes or moving objects.

It's a new kind of solitude you're experiencing, because you feel cut off from all the familiar things.

5. But not for long. A new world is opening up around you. Concentrate first on your ears. What do you hear? Count the sounds. How many separate ones can you identify? Listen for something unusual. Don't be turned off by the sound of traffic in the distance (or up close) or a neighbor's door slamming. Those are sounds of life too. I always have to smile when I hear an alarm clock ringing early in the morning. I know exactly how someone else is feeling. Listen for the ordinary things you're generally too busy to notice. When you hear a bird call, listen for the response. Sit quietly and wait. You'll hear the world breathing.

6. Now concentrate for a minute on your nose. How long has it been since you smelled the air of an August morning? Heavy with the scent of blooming things, touched with the fresh, grassy smell of somebody's newly mowed lawn, warmed by the sun, and moving softly, gently, not yet awake. Breathe normally, and, once or twice, breathe deeply. The heat of the summer day isn't upon you yet, but all the fragrance of a summer morning is there for the breathing.

7. It's time to talk about taste, which is a lot more than the ability to differentiate between sweet, sour, salty, and bitter. Did you know that you can actually taste things that haven't gone into your mouth? My friend Janet Somers went to the doctor and received an antibiotic injection in her arm. "What in the world is that bitter taste in my mouth?" she demanded. The doctor smiled. "The taste buds are so sensitive to bitterness that you're actually tasting the injection," he explained.

Taste is also a subjective thing, closely related to all our other sensory perceptions. The colors we see in our foods affect how we think they taste. We could eat blue oranges in the dark and enjoy them . . . until somebody turned on the lights.

The sense of smell is so closely related to taste that sometimes it's hard to separate the two. Bonnie Stuart was visiting her grandmother for the weekend. When she came in from playing in the backyard, there were two large loaves of banana bread baking in the warm oven. The little girl sniffed appreciatively. "Hmmmm . . . it smells so good. I can taste it already!" she exclaimed. How many of us have felt that way when we were waiting for the Thanksgiving turkey to come out of the oven?

Perhaps it's because "taste" means so many things to each of us that we've expanded the word to include the ability to appreciate what is beautiful. To taste is to have a sensation or experience of something. If people are able to "taste freedom" they can surely "taste" an August morning.

So when you're sitting out there with your eyes closed, let the smells and feelings and thoughts and visual images connect up with your total being. *Taste* the joy of being alive on an August morning.

8. Now I want you to feel. Use every nerve ending you possess to reach out and capture the sensations around you. Feel with your skin. Let the early morning air brush against your arms, your neck, your face. Tilt back your head and let the warmth cover your closed eyes. Wiggle your fingers, and your toes . . . stretch your arms above your head. Be aware that the air around you is not a stagnant thing. It moves constantly. Make yourself receptive to its currents.

Your five minutes are up. Are you ready for the big moment? Slowly open your eyes. Very slowly, because what you're going to see will be a shocker.

There it is. What can I say? It's your own private miracle . . . a little like being, for a moment, in the first garden. You're seeing, now, with more than your eyes, because all your other senses are still working overtime. The vividness, the newness, the purity of the world in focus is more than you had hoped for.

You've been away by yourself to the lonely place that Jesus spoke of. You've closed your eyes, the lamps of your body, and opened them again. The other day I read a

message in a Chinese fortune cookie. "The eye is blind if
the mind is absent," it said. Your eyes are no longer
blind, for your mind is back where it ought to be.

"Blessed are your eyes," said Jesus, "for they see . . ."
(Matthew 13:16). Right now, you're seeing better than you
ever have before.

Practice this technique for five minutes every morning
throughout the month of August. Then don't stop. Once
you've mastered the method, you can practice any day of
the year . . . whenever you need to improve your eyesight.

> *My eyes are tired, Lord!*
> *Let them rest.*
> *Show me how to see*
> *With the rest of me.*
> *Let me feel and taste*
> *And touch and hear*
> *Eternity on an August morning.*

9 SEPTEMBER
Too Busy to Be Bored

The proper function of man is to live, not to exist.
I shall not waste my days in trying to prolong them.
I shall use my time.

—Jack London

September is the back-to-school month. Although it's the traditional time for lots of moans and groans, it's also a time for shaking minds free of cobwebs, for putting thinking caps back on. I never knew a child who, despite all his protests, wasn't ready to go back to school in September. Vacation, glorious though it might have been, had lasted long enough. By the look and sound of the pent-up energy that abounds on the first back-to-school days, September probably rolls around just in time.

There's something special about these first autumn days. Yellow leaves crinkle and fall. The air turns crisp and cool. It's a perfect time for letting *your* pent-up energy loose. September is a month for living with enthusiasm.

Where, by the way, *is* your enthusiasm? You know, your zest for living, your interest in the things around you. Can you face September feeling, like Walt Whitman did, that "every hour of the light and dark is a miracle," or do you wake up in the mornings with about as much push as a limp fish? If you're finding yourself content to be a spectator to the greatest show on earth, you'd better answer the following question carefully.

What color is your life? Think about it, before you answer. Leave your favorite color out of it. Try to be as honest as you can. We humans have a tendency to attach colors to our emotions, you know. We have the blues, especially on Mondays. When our luck is down, things look black. We can be green with envy, and white as a sheet with fear. How about seeing red with anger, or being so embarrassed that you turn blushing pink? Yellow is usually a happy color, but what about gray? "It's a gray day." "He looked as gray as death." Not very uplifting thoughts, are they? That's because gray is a nothing color: neither white nor black, it sits on the fence and waits. It might as well be dead. Gray is the color of boredom. I hope it's not the color of your life.

All of us run the gamut of emotions. Given enough time, we're likely to touch them all. But if you find yourself giving in to one gray day after another, you're courting trouble. It's a sad fact that the more affluent our society becomes, the more people sit around complaining about nothing to do. When survival is no longer the prime concern of every day, our minds should turn to other activities. Sometimes, however, our imaginations seem to slip a cog, and we sit waiting for the inspiration that never comes.

Unfortunately, boredom isn't static. It feeds upon itself, growing larger and fatter until it earns enough names to look impressive. How about depression, hypertension, chronic fatigue, hypochondria? Do those sound interesting? How about the everyday ones like overweight, chewed fingernails, vague fears, vertigo, and irritability?

Now wait a minute. We all have those days when we get up in the morning with a vague feeling of wishing we could spend the day in a hammock with a good book. That's not the kind of boredom I'm talking about. That's a healthy rest stop.

But if your life is dull a little too often, if you get tired too soon, if the things you do are uninteresting, if you find yourself annoyed, even with those you love, and especially if you catch yourself sighing a lot (don't laugh . . . I don't know why women sigh when they're bored, but they do) you'd better read on.

A piece of you is definitely missing. An important piece, because you have an emptiness deep inside. Like Old Mother Hubbard, your cupboard is bare. Worse than that, it's a vacuum.

Unfortunately, you're not alone. In days when

smallpox is all but wiped out, and people get excited over
a case of measles, we have a new epidemic. But you can't
slap a bandage on boredom. It's more than a break in the
skin. There's no vaccination. There's no pat answer.

But I do have some clues. Call them guidelines, if you
want, and give them a try. Remember . . . there is not one
single thing about the world we live in that is boring.
Only your attitude toward it makes it unexciting. So take
the month of September to rid yourself of rust. Get your
creative gears oiled, and let your enthusiasm roll. Here's
how to break the boredom habit:

1. This first step is an important one. It's an
emergency measure. It gets you pointed immediately in
the right direction. The very next time you feel bored,
stop whatever it is that you've been doing, and do
something else.

Come on now! You can leave almost any job for a few
minutes. Unless you're performing surgery (in which case
you wouldn't be bored), break away, and try something
new. Anything. Go outside and walk around the house.
Play the piano. Clean the medicine cabinet. Bake a cake
and give it to a neighbor. Call a friend. Go somewhere on
the spur of the moment.

Now you have a head start on anti-boredom, but don't
stop. Busy-ness is not the whole answer. It's only the
beginning. Getting out of bed in the morning is just the
starting line for the race. It's necessary, of course, and
you'll feel better as soon as you do it, but it's not enough.
So move right on to the second step . . .

2. Come out of exile. Don't be like the squirrel who got
his seasons mixed up and hid in the tree trunk all
summer long. "Why do you stay cooped up in there?"
asked the woodchuck. "It's so exciting out here in the
world!"

The squirrel poked his nose out and looked around
carefully. "But it's so safe in here," he whispered. And it
was . . . until his food ran out!

It must have been boring, spending the whole glorious
summer in a tree trunk. But don't feel too sorry for that
squirrel. Boredom is a cop-out, an excuse for living. When

you turn your back on life, you always get backed into a corner.

Safety, you see, can't be your primary concern. Neither should a security blanket be your prized possession. We were made, like ships, to sail, not to sit at anchor in some snug harbor, or worse, in dry dock, with rusted hinges and chipped paint.

Don't you agree? Perhaps you're thinking of the person who said that we have to get rid of all our fears *before* we can begin to live. Well, that's not entirely true. Sometimes we get rid of our fears by *beginning* to live. The thing is, all of us have fears of one kind or another. We don't want them. We try to get rid of them. But the little devils seem to keep popping up. I'm not telling you to learn to live with them. They ought to be cleaned out as quickly as you can find the dustpan. But if you wait around for a completely clean house, you're going to spend a lot of time sweeping. My point is this: you have to get out there and live in *spite* of whatever it is you're afraid of.

Come out of your tree trunk, and splash right on in, just like the small boy who went to the beach. He didn't know the water was going to be so cold. But the chill didn't last. After a while, it even felt pretty good. Most important, cold water didn't keep him from splashing in again and again.

3. Have a survival kit. I can remember one Sunday, some years ago, when I was sitting next to our youngest son in church. No matter how quietly he tried to move, he crackled. It wasn't until later that I discovered his pants pockets were stuffed with edibles and his coat was lined with comic books. "At least," my husband said, "he came prepared."

Your survival kit doesn't have to be that drastic. I think a list will be enough. Write down all the things you really want to do, but have never had the time (or courage) to try. I have a friend named Elizabeth who started a list like that years ago. She keeps it in a drawer as a reminder that there's plenty left out there in the world for her to explore. This year she summoned up her

courage and took a glider ride as a birthday gift from her
family. What will she do when all the items are checked
off? She's not worried about that. Her "survival kit" list
is better than a wish book, because it doesn't have a last
page. With enthusiasm like hers, the list will grow and
grow. And you can bet that looking forward to each new
experience goes a long way toward burying boredom.

If you want something more concrete than a list, be
ready with a large box. Fill it as you go along with
things you want to do: that special book you've been
wanting to read; a piece of material you can make into a
long-awaited evening skirt; a stack of pretty cards to
write on and send to friends; a pillow cover to embroider;
a package of seeds to plant. There is only one restriction
on your survival kit. These must be things you really
want to do. You should feel that you can hardly wait. If
you're still bored when you're busy, you're not busy at the
right kind of things. You made the choices; you have no
one to blame but yourself.

4. Carry a mental compass. Know your directions:
enthusiasm is up; depression is down.

We used to think, thanks to Newton and his falling
apple, that the law of gravity was infallible. What goes
up, must come down. Isn't that what we were taught?
Too bad Newton couldn't have lived long enough to see
the age of space travel, when what goes up sometimes
stays up forever.

That's the way your attitude about life should be. As
high as the sky, with no need for falling. Remember the
story of Chicken Little, who went around announcing
that the sky was falling? What a gloom machine he
must have been. Children love the story, because it is so
ridiculous. In their innate wisdom, they wonder who in
the world would spend his days waiting for the sky to fall
in. Some of us adults do.

How wise to see things like the little boy who gazed up
at the altar and asked, "What's that big plus sign doing
up there?" He recognized the cross as a positive symbol.
His mental compass was right on target.

Where's *your* mental compass? Make your choice. Don't

be like the crooked man who built a crooked house. Once
he got started, everything he did was crooked. He didn't
have any sense of direction at all.

5. Get in there and hustle! If you don't, you're liable to
become a dull person. That's what happened to Ann
Murphy. I watched her as she sat one morning in her
kitchen, her elbows on the sill, while she stared out the
window.

"I never should have poured the coffee," she
complained. "I should have left it in the pot until it had
oily film on top. I should have gone to Siberia on a fast
plane. It's been that kind of morning."

"What on earth happened?" I asked. From her tone, I
expected the worst.

"Nothing!" she muttered. "Nothing ever happens.
That's the trouble. I got up and poured the coffee, and
everybody else got up and grumbled around the way they
always do." She looked at me with tear-filled eyes. "Is
this it? Is this all I can expect from life?"

My answer could only be, "Yes. That's all there is . . . if
you stop right there and go back to bed, that's all you
can expect out of life."

Ann was a gray person. The only way to break out of
her nest of boredom was to get out and hustle. I told her
so. At first she looked insulted.

"How?" she demanded.

I couldn't help laughing. "A good place to start is by
getting out of your chair," I said. Ann didn't know that
life wasn't passing out favors. She didn't realize that if
you want hot tamales, you have to add some chili to the
sauce!

About one hundred years ago, a man named Josiah
Gilbert Holland had a few choice words to say on the
matter of getting out and hustling.

> *God gives every bird his food,*
> *but He does not throw it into the nest.*

By the way, did you ever see a bored bird? I did, only
once. For some reason he took a liking to our bedroom

window. He came every day that spring, arriving about 4:30 A.M. to peck at the glass. He kept it up until mid-afternoon, when he began collecting bits of straw and leaves, which he tried to apply to the window's surface. Of course, everything dropped to the ground. He never accomplished a thing. And . . . listen to this . . . he never tried a new tactic. Toward the end of the season, he was beginning to lose his feathers, his eyes looked glazed, his head drooped. Like Ann Murphy, he probably wondered if this was it! All the equipment was available. He just couldn't seem to put things together.

You can't just sit through life and expect everything to come up roses. Ecclesiastes puts it this way: "Whatever your hand finds to do, do it with your might" (9:10). This doesn't include moping at the kitchen window or dropping loose straw on the ground.

It does include having a workable goal. Only when you have a definite aim in sight, so that you can place your feet firmly on the stepping-stones of productivity, is your busy-ness going to keep you vitalized. It's no good being as busy as a bee unless you produce a little honey. It's no good collecting straw unless you eventually come up with a nest.

6. Be a people watcher. It's a wonderful way to jerk yourself up by the bootstraps. Just look at the faces around you. How many look preoccupied, disinterested . . . bored? How many look vital and alive, their faces animated, their eyes sparkling? Watch them all. Try to imagine what makes people look the way they do. Discover the infinite variety of the human countenance. Then ask yourself what *you* look like. Is your mouth turned up in a smile? Or sagging at the corners? Are you staring blankly . . . or are you looking at what you see? If you can decide which way you *want* to look, it's five spare minutes well spent.

7. Don't *be* a bore. I wish I could have met the man who said, "The man who rows the boat generally doesn't have time to rock it." Show me a troublemaker, and I'll show you a bored person. The sad fact is that most bored people soon become bores. You never catch one picking

up an oar. They're too busy thinking about themselves.
Watch for these warning signals in *yourself*:

> *A bore talks when he should listen.*
> *A bore nags.*
> *A bore is selfish.*
> *A bore turns his back on life, but is interested in*
>   *your business.*

Watch for the red light. Don't let yourself fall into the
boredom trap. Be a rower, not a rocker.

8. Stop looking out at the world through dirty windows.
Here's a little exercise to help you. Pick an object, any
object. Anything from a bowl of sugar to a picket fence.
Stare at it. Let its edges grow hazy. Let your eyes go out
of focus. Exciting? Not very. Can you imagine how you
look? That's not very exciting either. Now, pull yourself
back into focus and have a good look at that bowl of
sugar or picket fence. Concentrate on its fine points. Keep
your vision edges sharp. Can you *feel* the difference?
Notice how your eyes are actually moving, even darting,
as they take in the smallest details. If you could see
yourself now, you'd *notice* a difference.

Remember this experiment the next time you're bored.
You alone can wipe your dirty windows clean. Don't stare
blankly; it fogs your windows. Try looking at things
around you with interest and enthusiasm, and wipe the
glass clean.

9. Be good for something. "But I try to be a good
person," I can hear you saying. "Isn't that enough? I
make a real effort to do all the right things. I don't rob,
lie, cheat, or steal!"

So why do you get bored? Henry David Thoreau tells it
the way it is: "Be not simply good . . . be good for
something." Doesn't that imply more than good
behavior? Of course it does! It implies action. It implies
purpose.

The key word is *change.* I'm reminded of the
woodcarver I once watched for a long period of time. The
artist was so talented that, as the shape of the figure

emerged, I could have sworn that it had been there all along, and all the artisan had to do was strip away the extra covering. It looked so easy, the change he created. But it wasn't a hit-and-miss affair. It involved, he told me, visualizing the total result before beginning. It also involved his total commitment. In other words, he didn't just hack away at the life of his wood. He had a plan, and he was part of it.

You can be a moving force, an impetus. You can change things. If you can't think of anything else for starters, why not move the furniture and put a fresh bouquet on the coffee table. That's change, and it involves you—because you're a little different each time you act. How ambitious are you? Write a letter to the editor. Join the church choir. Run for office. Wherever you go, make your presence felt.

Hans Christian Andersen had a wonderful philosophy. "To be of use in this world," he believed, "is the only way to be happy." Take a tip from him and make yourself useful. Don't turn your back on life. Stand right up and be counted. You'll never be the same again.

10. Use it or lose it. I'm talking about life. Approach it with enthusiasm. It's the only way anything good gets done. Never crawl into a tree trunk to hide. Instead, "Let your light so shine before men, that they may see your good works and give glory to your Father who is in heaven" (Matthew 5:16).

Life's a little like love. The more you spend, the more there is. And it's a little like a kiss. It's more fun when you share it. So take your pent-up energy and spend it on the month of September. Put on your thinking cap and let imagination flow. Fight boredom with action, and it won't have a chance to thrive. Know that every hour *is* a miracle. How can you be bored with that?

> *Thank you, Father, for the*
> *Crisp, sweet air of September,*
> *That opens our hearts to*

Living.
Help our lights to shine, that
All good works
May glorify thy name.

10 OCTOBER
Laugh Along with God

Mirth is like a flash of lightning, that breaks
through a gloom of clouds, and glitters for a
moment . . . a kind of daylight in the mind . . .
                                        —Joseph Addison

Listen; you may be allowed
To hear my laughter from a cloud.
                              —Sir Walter Raleigh

This morning I took my coffee to the patio. It was still
early . . . seven o'clock, to be exact. My husband was just
getting up. The children had snatched their lunches and
dashed down the long hill to the schoolbus.

So far, the day had been nothing to shout about. Little
things had gone wrong, putting frowns on usually
cheerful faces. If this is the way it's starting out, I
grumbled, I wonder if it wouldn't be better to go back to
bed. That's when I took my coffee to the patio. To be
alone and start the morning over. And I was, for all
practical purposes, alone. Well, not quite. There were the
sow bugs.

I reached down to pull a prickly weed from the roses
and unearthed them. They scrambled wildly, then rolled
up into smug little gray balls like pigs on their backs, or
like hedgehogs in the croquet game in *Alice in
Wonderland*. I watched them a minute, shiny clowns in
gray armor, tumbling in the dirt.

How God must have laughed, I thought, when he made
a sow bug. To my surprise, I was smiling.

The leaves of the evergreen pear tree rustled and
swayed, their ruffled edges catching the sunlight and
rubbing against the branches like busy fingers. The noise

they made was like an echo. I couldn't put my finger on
it, but it was a happy sound.

One branch dipped suddenly with added weight, and I
saw the gray and white feathers of the neighborhood
mockingbird, that curious creature with no voice of its
own. He hopped closer and cocked his head. *"Mee-ow!"* he
said, and looked me in the eye. I grinned back at him. I
couldn't help it. He might not know what he was
supposed to sound like, but he had the courage of a
rooster.

How God must have chuckled, I thought, when he
made a mockingbird.

I had turned to carry my empty cup into the house,
when I spied the praying mantis. I almost missed it, for
it rose like a green leaf with dew on its head, clinging to
the brown stem with its twiggy legs. It reminded me of
something you could make out of Tinker Toys: little men
and animals with interchangeable parts. I put out a
finger tentatively, and it raised angry wings, making a
brilliant, lavender display with large, fake eyes flapping
in my direction. I laughed aloud.

"God," I said, "you really let yourself go when you
made this one." I'd felt the same way myself when,
decorating Christmas cookies, I'd made a few nonsense
ones at the end of the batch.

The pines on the hill whispered like soft rain. I stopped
a moment and listened to the wind, and I knew I was
smiling as I opened the door and went back into the
house. It hadn't started out as such a great morning, but
somehow it had changed. God reveals himself in many
ways; I'd always known that. But this morning he did a
little extra. He shared with me his laughter.

Perhaps it's a coincidence that this happened in the
month of October. But I don't think so. There is nothing
sorrowful about this month. It clicks its heels and laughs
aloud. It teases and tempts, daring you not to smile.
October has a sense of humor. It's the perfect time to
listen for the sounds of God's laughter. It waits for you in
unexpected places, and it's worth the search. He shares it

willingly; all we have to do is lift up our hearts and listen.

Wait a minute! Didn't anyone ever tell you that God has a sense of humor? Why, then, do you think he made a smile? If your vision of God is that of a white-haired patriarch, scowling from some faroff cloud . . . forget it. God is here, right now, with you and me. And he knows how to smile. His laughter lights up the skies. Sometimes it's gentle, like a twilight rain. Sometimes it's as silent as the wings of a butterfly, brushing the petal of a flower. When you learn to recognize it . . . when you know that God is laughing with you . . . you'll add a new dimension to your life.

Why do we laugh anyway? The reasons are countless, but let's name a few. We laugh for joy. Spread wide your arms and laugh in the sun. Lift up your face and also laugh in the rain. Laugh for the joy of wind in your face. Laugh for the pure happiness of being alive.

We laugh to add zest to our days. Laughter is the spice that makes life full-flavored. Any good cook knows that seasoning is, after all, a lot more than salt. And laughter, unlike other additives, is harmless. Have you ever heard of anyone who died of laughter? No. But you and I both know a lot of people who felt better because of it.

We laugh because we can't help it. Sometimes the reason is obvious. Other times we don't know why. When your funny bone tickles, the corners of your mouth turn up. Don't analyze it; just enjoy it.

We laugh because it's contagious; it's true that when you laugh, the world laughs with you. It's like a chain reaction, but it has to start with you. Lots of other things are contagious too, like the common cold. So for pity's sake, let it be laughter that you spread around.

Sometimes laughter catches you by surprise. It was the late John Barrymore who said that "happiness sneaks in through a door you didn't know you had left open." So does laughter. Let it sneak up on you through that open door. Welcome it. Respond to it. It's a gift without a price tag.

Take time to laugh in the month of October. If you're
out of practice, learn again. It's a step-by-step process.
You can't appreciate humor around you until you can
find the humor *in* you. You can't laugh with others until
you can laugh at yourself. You can't laugh along with
God until you learn to recognize his humor in the world
around you.

Let's take it in four easy stages. *First,* you've got to
learn to laugh at yourself. There was once a children's
book about a hero called Tinker Town Tom. The villain
of the story was a terrible white-faced clown who wore a
turned-down mouth and an awful scowl. He was so glum
that he was funny. Children looked at his pictures and
collapsed with laughter. Try reacting the same way next
time you look in the mirror and see a glum face looking
back. Laugh at yourself, and, while you're at it, learn to
smile at your mistakes. Brush yourself off and give life
another try.

Find something each morning that you can smile
about. Do it before you get out of bed. How do you feel
this morning? Do you have to keep propping open your
eyes? Is your body racked with all sorts of symptoms,
real or imaginary? Do you absolutely know that you can't
stand up?

Have you ever seen a teen-ager get up in the morning,
groaning and groping his way unwillingly back into life?
Laughable, isn't it? Be honest. You were pretty laughable
this morning, too.

Second, learn to see humor in the world around you.
Look out your window and watch that little cloud,
fighting a losing battle over keeping its shape. You've
been doing the same thing for years. It's called the diet
game. Isn't that worth a smile?

See those two birds on the telephone wire? They're not
just sitting there. They're on the lookout for the early
morning worm. Can you imagine getting up early in the
morning for a breakfast like that? Isn't it worth a
chuckle?

The small town where I grew up still talks about the
hot Sunday in August when a small white dog came to

church. Reverend Baker was doing his best and, unfortunately, his longest. Heads nodded. Mothers worried about dinners getting crisp around the edges. Beads of moisture tickled wet paths down the backs of warm necks. People crossed their legs and uncrossed them again. Oblivious, the Reverend droned on. Suddenly, he stopped and stared down the center aisle. All eyes that were still open followed his, and moved slowly forward as a small, white, breedless dog trotted toward him and sat, just beneath the pulpit, with one ear cocked and a short tail thumping the wooden floor. The tension was broken, the monotony erased. A good laugh saved the day.

Third, learn to laugh with others. Deborah Johnson was watching her young daughter play in the yard. Everything was fine until the family pet, a Saint Bernard with a tongue the size of a dinner plate, came up close to the little girl and affectionately lapped her face clean.

The child screwed up her mouth in such a comic expression of distaste that Deborah burst out laughing. Seeing that her reaction had distressed her daughter, she quickly put her arms around the little girl and reassured her. "I'm not laughing *at* you; I'm laughing *with* you," she declared. It didn't take long for her daughter to smile. She'd learned to laugh at herself, because her mother laughed with her.

There's an important difference. Derisive laughter . . . laughing *at* someone . . . is a destructive thing. It's not really laughter at all, but a lonely sound, hollow and harmful. Laughing *with* someone is nourishing. It reaches out and embraces. It's a joyful sharing.

Deborah Johnson said, "I'm laughing with you, not at you." Isn't that how God feels about *his* children? He laughs with us whenever we are perceptive enough to join him. Sometimes he laughs alone, because we're too busy, or too solemn, to sense the humor around us. But he does laugh.

The *fourth,* and obvious thing you need to do is to laugh along with God. Listen for his voice in the laughter of children playing in the grass. Watch for his humor in dancing leaves, in the rainbow that has no end, in the pink camellia bush that sports one white flower. Look for his smile in an early morning sky. Listen to the sound of rain, and the whisper of snowflakes. Hear his voice as it gathers the wind.

If you let one day pass without laughter, you've let one day pass that could have been a better day. Laugh gently, laugh loudly, laugh happily, laugh kindly. Don't just stand there. Laugh along with God.

> *Thank you, Lord, for the gift of mirth,*
> *For the sounds of laughter*
> *And the happiness that comes with a smile.*
> *Laugh with me, Lord, and*
> *Show me how to listen*
> *For the sounds of laughter*
> *In your voice.*

11 NOVEMBER
Break the People Barrier

Don't walk in front of me ... I may not follow.
Don't walk behind me ... I may not lead.
Walk beside me ...
  And just be my friend.
                              —Albert Camus

  I am a human being.
  Nothing human can be alien to me.
                    —ancient philosopher

God believes in a technicolor world. He proved it by
giving us November. It's a month that belongs on an
artist's palette, where all the colors are dabbled, one by
one, then blended until the surface is a blaze of color. In
November I like to stand ankle-deep in crimson leaves
and feel the wind on my face. The world is my
kaleidoscope, turning slowly, revealing the blaze of glory
which is autumn.

We can learn a lot from November. It's a time for giving thanks, a season of ripeness, when crops are gathered
in. It's also a month which shouts of the endless variety
of life. It's an ideal time to consider the endless variety
of *people*.

I'm talking about color, and size, and shape, and age,
and whatever else there is about us that makes us
different from each other. What a dull world it would be
if we were all the same. In his infinite wisdom, God
understood. Until *you* understand, until *you* open your
heart to embrace the differences of other human beings,
there's something missing in your life. It's that special
ability to reach out with your mind and touch the mind
of another human being. Without it, you walk alone.

So let's take the month of November and use it to

break the people barrier. Open wide your doors and windows. I mean it literally. Go from room to room and open them all. Give your house a good healthy fresh-airing. How long has it been since you were aware that from each window of your house you can see a completely different picture?

Open a door or window every morning of this month and take a few seconds to look out. Listen to the sound of the handle turning. It's like a quiet invitation. Now close that same door and hear the difference. There is no sound in the world quite as final as the sound of a shutting door. I'm not ready to be isolated like that. Are you?

Of course not! So open the doors of your house and the windows of your mind. Reach out right this minute, and lift the latch. The people barrier is begging to be broken.

Let's talk first about color. I'm not referring to autumn leaves. I'm talking about skin. Yours and mine. I'll never forget the time I overheard a mother telling her small son what to do when he saw someone whose skin was different from his own.

"Just pretend you didn't notice," she advised.

He looked up at her and frowned. "How?" he asked. "I can't look at him without seeing him!"

Wise words. Let's go one step further. You *shouldn't* look at somebody without seeing him. If his appearance is different from yours, so much the better. How would you like to look in the mirror every morning and see the face of your neighbor down the street?

You don't think that's such a great idea, do you? You're glad God made our faces different. Why, then, should he have done any less with our skins? I once heard someone comment that the only way to solve the prejudice problem was to make everyone the same color, preferably gray. Now how would you like *that?*

Personally, I'm willing to settle for technicolor. What would the month of November be if the world turned gray, instead of scarlet and gold? I'll tell you what it would be like.

Drab. Uninteresting. Depressing.

God gave us November for a perfectly good reason. So

that we could enjoy its infinite variety. Why not apply
the same reasoning to our enjoyment of people? Let's
rejoice in our differences. We already have in common
our humanity.

I can think of *one* difference that always gets more
groans than cheers. It's age difference, and I'm happy to
tell you that its problems are grossly overrated. All the
trouble began, I think, when somebody tacked a label on
it and called it the "generation gap."

Those two words instill fear in the hardiest heart and
insecurity in the stablest soul. Why? Because whatever
age you are, it's probably the wrong one. You always
need to be a few years younger or a few years older.
Since you aren't, you're caught on a tightrope of
misunderstanding, where you constantly must teeter,
waiting to fall.

That's what they'd *like* you to believe! The generation
gap is nothing more than a few years between your
birthday and mine. How do you jump across it? You
don't have to. It's only a small puddle in time. You can
step right over without even getting your feet wet. Here's
how:

1. Think about caterpillars.
2. Take down the quarantines.

Maybe I'd better do a little explaining. First, let's talk
about caterpillars. We human beings are a little like
them, you know. We don't go to sleep in cocoons, but the
metamorphosis is often just as complete. Someone once
said that a child is "someone who passes through your
life and then disappears into an adult."

The author of Ecclesiastes must have been thinking
along those same lines. "For everything there is a season,
and a time for every matter under heaven" (3:1). There's
a time for youth and a time for age in each of our lives.
Look at it this way: if all the leaves of all the trees stayed
green and fresh forever, we would have to take November
off the calendar. What a dull place the world would be
without the glory of autumn. What a loss of beauty we
would suffer if caterpillars never became butterflies.

Growing up and aging are not one and the same.

Think of life, instead, as a series of stages. As long as we live, we're always entering a new one.

All mothers know this for a fact. Nora Clarke put it into her own words when she looked at her young son and shook her head in exasperation. "He's just in a stage," she said. Not too many years later, he entered his teens, and Nora was heard to comment, "I just got my strength back from the last stage, and I'm afraid he's entering a new one."

We learn, and we grow, and we change. But, just like the butterfly, we do it day by day, not in ten-year strides. More often than not, we do a lot of overlapping. The important thing to remember is that you've either been there, or you're on your way. That so-called "generation gap" is not a giant chasm that keeps us apart. It's nothing more than a small puddle in the road, and you already have one foot across.

Step right on over. All you have to do is pull down the quarantines. You know what I mean . . . stop isolating yourself from other age groups. It's just as unnatural as making all tall men live on the same side of town.

When I was a child, I spent my summers in a household that boasted four generations under one roof. Of course there was occasional friction, but that happens in every family, regardless of age spans. Believe it or not, I remember those summers with nothing but fondness. Not everyone can duplicate this kind of experience. I was one of the lucky ones. I found out then how much children can learn from grandparents and great aunts and uncles and even from elderly neighbors. And I know now that it's a two-sided coin. You and I can always learn something new from a child.

Children keep us young, even though we sometimes think they'll be the death of us. We adults help children mature, even though they *know* we'll be the death of them!

Sure, the noise of small children can get on your nerves, but have you forgotten what it was like to feel the excitement of a child? Can you sit on your porch and watch schoolchildren coming and going and enjoy the sounds of their voices? Or do you want to go inside and shut the door? Can you go to a rest home and take the wrinkled hand of a stranger and remember that this was once a child, and still is . . . a child of God? Can you try?

A recent newspaper article caught my eye. The headline read something like this: RETIREMENT COMMUNITY SEEKS TO BAR CHILDREN. Legal? Probably. Protection of privacy? Undoubtedly. Sad? You bet your life! There's nothing sadder than voluntary isolation.

I showed the article to an elderly neighbor. She read it and shook her head. "That's quite a price for peace and quiet," she said as she smiled. Then she had to excuse herself and take a tray of golden oatmeal cookies from the oven. She liked to bake them fresh, she said, for any children who happened by. And they did happen by. Often.

Did they bother her? Was the noisy chatter too much? "Sometimes." She laughed. "But then I just tell them I'm tired and need to rest a little while. They always leave quietly, and they always come back. I think," she added, with a twinkle, "that they're addicted to oatmeal."

They were addicted, all right, but oatmeal didn't have a thing to do with it. They were addicted to companionship. After all, who can better understand a child than someone who has been one? The trouble is, we tend to forget. And we forget much quicker when we aren't reminded. Small children are the best reminders. They aren't picky. They know a friend when they see one, and age doesn't bother them at all. The only thing that bothers them . . . and the rest of us . . . is being shut out.

If you associate only with people of your own age, you'll never get your missing parts together, and I'll tell you why. People are a lot like film. The quality of the finished picture depends to a great extent on the right amount of exposure.

The truth of the matter is . . . people need people. All sorts of people. "Man is a special being," said Daniel Webster, ". . . and if left to himself in an isolated condition, would be one of the weakest creatures, but associated with his kind, he works wonders." His "kind" doesn't mean appearance or age. It means *human* kind. That covers a lot of territory.

I once knew an independent soul named Faye Simpson. She had a little trouble accepting this idea of common need. "People are too darned much trouble!" she stormed one day. "I'd be better off having a relationship with a fence post!" She was right on one account. A fence post probably wouldn't give Faye much trouble. But she'd overlooked something basic. It wouldn't do much *for* her either.

Don't be like Faye. *Refuse* to put a fence around your mind. Expose yourself instead. Open the door to people every day. Here are seven basic rules to follow. Take them one at a time . . . one item a day. When the first week is over, start from the beginning. By the end of November, you'll be an expert. Start now. It's not too late to break the people barrier.

1. Be available when someone needs you. Do you remember the old bravery game we used to play? I'm not sure whether we did it to prove our fearlessness or our foolishness, but it involved standing with your back to someone and letting yourself fall straight back until, hopefully, your friend would catch you just before you touched the floor. How many people trust *you* that well? Be a friend today by catching someone before he falls.

2. Say something nice to somebody. Mark Twain said that he could "live for two months on a good compliment." I think we all could. Be generous. Hand out at least one compliment today.

3. Don't be afraid of being vulnerable. You'll be surprised how nice people are going to be. When you finally decide to open up your life to people, it's like looking up through a skylight, straight into infinity.

4. Forgive. The size of the grievance isn't important. What's important is that you should forgive completely. Don't wait for compensation; just wipe your score sheet clean. Go ahead and bury the hatchet, then forget where you dug the hole.

5. Remember to have a sense of humor. Face it, no

matter how hard you try, no matter how admirable your intentions, some days just don't go the way they're planned. People, bless them, *can* be irritating. Once in a while it might seem like they're not cooperating at all. Don't be discouraged. You haven't had to walk in their shoes. You don't have any idea what difficulties they may be facing. Have patience, and keep your smile handy. I saw these words written on a sign on a classroom wall. "When you're ready to go off the edge . . . remember that the Lord, in his infinite mercy, made the world round." Remember . . . you *can* afford to smile.

6. Talk to someone who is not in your age group. Speak to someone younger. Visit with someone older. A well-known actress was heard to say that she wanted to play many age roles, because the variety helped her grow as an actress. I'll bet it also helped her grow as a human being.

7. Train your eyes to look for color. Watch for it in nature; observe it in your everyday life; see it in the faces of other people. Be glad you live in a technicolor world.

Remember this: each one of us is capable of casting a giant shadow. But who wants to live in a shadow world? "It's great to be great," said Will Rogers, "but it's greater to be human." Human beings . . . of all shapes and ages . . . are colorful people. Go ahead and cast your shadow. Cast it long, and cast it straight. But let it be the only thing about you that is gray!

> *Thank you, Lord, for the glory of autumn,*
> *For crisp, crimson leaves*
> *Dancing color on the wind.*
> *Tune our hearts to the variety*
> *Called life,*
> *That we may reach out to others*
> *Through the open skylights*
> *Of our minds.*

12 DECEMBER
Take a Coffee Break with God

More things are wrought by prayer
Than this world dreams of.
    —Tennyson *Morte D'Arthur*

... speak to God as if men were listening.
                    —Seneca

When the first of December rolls around, I feel as if a curtain is going up. I tingle with the excitement and anticipation of a first-night performance, when my seat is in the front row. I know it's going to be the same old story, but that's the miracle of the Christmas season: the same old story is always new.

December *is* a month of miracles. From the first day to the last, special things happen. One of the most special is that we take time to think about each other. And we communicate. Oh, how we communicate! Ask any mailman if you don't believe me. December is the month for taking time out and letting your friends know you're alive. Cards ... greetings ... letters ... don't pretend you're not happy when they come to *your* house.

But the mailbox isn't the only way we have of speaking to each other. There is something about the Christmas season that loosens our tongues. We even speak to strangers, wishing them happiness. "Merry Christmas!" is more than a greeting. It's a way we have of talking to each other.

What a perfect time of year to practice talking to God! Let's take the month of December and polish up our communication techniques. Most people call it prayer, and that's all right with me. Just don't be surprised when it's not quite what you expected.

I have this theory, you see, that talking with God

involves a lot more than closing your eyes and sitting in the dark. I'm afraid that's what we teach children to do. Fortunately, children are sensible people, and many of them instinctively know better. Listen to this story:

Tommy Johnson knelt by his bed and put his hands up, palms together. "Now I lay me down to sleep," he chanted.

"Wait a minute," interrupted his mother. "You have to close your eyes."

"Why?"

Mrs. Johnson faltered. "That's the way you pray. You have to start by closing your eyes."

"Then I can't *see* anything," protested Tommy. "What's so good about praying in the dark?"

He had a point. Would you talk to your best friend with your eyes shut? Of course not. You'd have them wide open. Why, then, would you want to do less when you speak with God?

Do you remember, 'way back in August, when I told you all about the value of closing your eyes? Good, because now I'm turning right around and telling you to open them. Am I contradicting myself? Not at all! Closing your eyes was a good and necessary exercise, but you'll remember that I said you only needed to spend a few minutes a day at it.

Now it's time to open them wide . . . and keep them open when you pray. I'm not talking about meditation, that quiet time when you see with your inner eye. You meditate by yourself, but you pray by talking to God. It's probably the finest kind of worship, and you can do it with your eyes wide open.

What's that? You never did it that way before? So much the better. It's time you got up off your knees and tried something new. You won't be sorry, and neither will God. Quite frankly, when I close my eyes at night and try to talk to God, the two of us don't get much said, because I fall asleep. When we bow our heads and pray in church, it's a community effort. Very worthwhile, but not enough. And when we sit around the kitchen table

and ask for God's blessing, I'm ashamed to admit that
my mind is on a thousand dinnertime details.

Those occasions, with all due respect, are what I call
times of thoughtless praying. Now hold on! Before you go
to pieces, let me explain. Many times when we sit down
and close our eyes, we really don't "get it all together."
We either let somebody else do the talking for us, or we
simply sit and rest. There's nothing really wrong with
that, as long as it's *sometimes.* But if you never go any
farther . . . if you never let your own self get involved . . .
then you remind me of the woman who took a bottle and
sealed her name inside, then tossed it out into the ocean,
with the hope that the tide would eventually deposit it
somewhere. That's what I call a prime example of really
halfhearted communication. It's not far removed from
thoughtless praying.

You might agree to go along with me this far, but I'll
bet you're wondering what getting involved has to do
with opening your eyes. Let me give you some concrete
examples.

One day I was hiking with my friend Sarah Peterson
in the foothills. A red-winged blackbird cawed loudly and
lifted out of the cattail swamp. It swooped low over
Sarah's head, showing its glistening black and red finery.
She was so touched that she closed her eyes on the spot
and thanked the Lord for the beauty of nature. At the
risk of seeming irreverent, I'll admit that I had
something better to do. If Sarah had kept her eyes open,
she would have seen that bird fly back to the nest and
feed breakfast to a crew of hungry babies. It was a sight
I'll never forget, and I had the distinct feeling that God
wanted to shout: "Keep those eyes open. There's a whole
world out there to see!"

My neighbor down the road has chosen a unique place
to be thankful. Thelma likes to pray at the kitchen sink.
It all started one morning, she told me, when she was
standing, elbow-deep in dirty dishwater. She glanced out
the window and saw two ruby-throated hummingbirds
taking turns on their tiny nest. It was no bigger than

half a walnut, and they had built it for the second year in a row, right outside her kitchen window, where it was shaded by the thick Oregon Grape bushes. She would never have seen the nest if she hadn't been standing there swishing soap suds. Right then and there, she decided to thank God for her kitchen sink and a lot of other perfectly ordinary things.

Thelma never closed her eyes. She didn't dare. She was perfectly aware of what she might miss. Opening her eyes didn't decrease her reverence one bit. It just widened her vision. Your world, you see, is just as big as you allow it to be. Even if you have a hard time getting out of the kitchen, your vision can encompass much more than the dishrag. Your eye for beauty can be perceptive wherever you are . . . but only if you keep it open.

When Jesus spoke to God in a garden and said, ". . . not my will, but thine, be done . . ." he spoke in the darkness. But I have a feeling that his eyes were wide open. Now here's something for you to think about: how do we know what he said to God, unless he spoke the words so that someone else could hear them? That's right . . . said them right out loud. Why not? Is there some kind of rule that says only silent prayers will be heard?

Unless you've recently joined a monastic order that requires total silence, or have a severe communicative disorder, you are one among the millions of human beings who start your day by opening your mouth and speaking. I'm talking about *words*. Combinations of sounds that have meaning. Those lilting, sonorous, sometimes guttural, but often gliding noises that lift us above the beasts and let us communicate with each other.

Why not with God? Because, you're probably insisting, it isn't necessary. God hears our thoughts before we put them into words. You're absolutely right. He does. And it probably *isn't* necessary for you to speak out loud . . . not for God. But it *is,* at least sometimes, quite necessary for you and for me.

One day, quite by accident, I discovered how to talk out loud to God. Let me tell you about it.

I had been waving good morning to Jennie Stewart for

two weeks. She was a new neighbor, but as we both had large families, waving was all we'd had time for. This morning, I determined to pay her a visit. I didn't know that the short walk between our two houses would change my life.

I knocked lightly on the kitchen door. She evidently had other company. I could hear her talking to someone and was about to leave, when the voices stopped, and she called for me to come in.

I pushed open the door. "I didn't mean to interrupt . . ." I began, and stopped, confused. She was sitting at her kitchen table. A cup of coffee was in front of her. She was alone.

"You're not interrupting," she smiled. "Come on in."

"I must be hearing things. I thought I heard you talking to someone."

"You did. I was taking a coffee break with God."

My mouth must have dropped open, for she laughed. "Why don't you try it sometime?" she suggested. "It beats prayer all to pieces." It was like sitting in the face of sacrilege. I'd been brought up on formal prayer, and there were some things you just didn't joke about. Jennie Stewart was a lovely woman, but she had some strange ideas!

That was one coffee break I'll never forget, for those strange ideas wouldn't seem to leave me alone. Her words came back to me day after day. "Why don't you try it sometime?" she had asked.

When time came in my daily schedule for a breather from work, I would plug in the coffee, reach for a cup, and think of Jennie Stewart. Then I'd think of some excuse and not bother to sit down at all. This only happened when I was alone. When a friend dropped by, the coffee pot perked, and our tongues waggled. But I seemed incapable of facing the kitchen table all by myself. I had almost given up drinking coffee alone because of the uncomfortable feeling it gave me. Then one day a good friend, harried and tired from a day with sick children, stepped into my kitchen.

"Do you have a few minutes?" she asked.

"Sure. Sit down. You look like you could use a cup of coffee."

"Oh," she smiled, "I just need to sit down quietly and talk to someone."

There it was. The words were out. There was no need like the need to talk to someone. Maybe this was what prayer was all about. Jennie Stewart had discovered the difference between communication with God and wasted word power.

Had I become so tangled in the discipline of formal prayer that I was afraid to talk to God all by myself? I couldn't wait to find out. When I was alone, I sat at the kitchen table. I wondered how to start. Memorized lines popped in and out of my head.

"Our Father . . . Now I lay me down to sleep . . . Forgive us our debts . . ." Every prayer I'd ever known tried to find its way. Even phrases from hymns filled my mind. How easy, I thought, to recite a poem and let it go at that. Then I remembered the voices I had thought I'd overheard at the "coffee break" that day. Perhaps it was too hard to organize your thoughts in silence. Maybe you had to speak out loud, just as if you were visiting with a friend. Was this the way to marshal wandering thoughts and organize words so that the important things finally got said?

"Dear Lord," I began, and stopped. It was too much like writing a letter to Santa.

I looked furtively around me to make sure I was alone. I even latched the kitchen door. Slightly embarrassed, I sat down at the table and cleared my throat. "Well, God," I whispered, "here we are."

From there on, it was easy. The words came quickly, and the silences were full of peaceful thoughts. When I thought of something to say, I said it. In between, I learned to listen. We rambled on about lots of things, God and I, about people we both knew, in a language we both could understand. It was like a wonderful, restful visit with an old friend.

I never prayed again by myself. I invited God into my kitchen. Invite God into *your* kitchen. Do it every

morning in the month of December. You may stutter a
little at first, but you'll find that the words soon come
easier, and that your thoughts are clearer than ever
before. Do you need a few guidelines to get started? Try
these:

1. Turn to Matthew 6:9-13, and study the example. The
Lord's Prayer says it well, but Jesus didn't intend for us
to stop there. "Pray *like* this," he said, knowing full well
the necessity of speaking personally, in your own words.
Use this prayer as a guide, but don't recite it as if it were
a nursery rhyme.

2. Take your time. Don't try to get all your thoughts
out in one big mouthful. Do you remember the story of
the small boy who was rushing frantically to finish his
math before the bell rang? Finally, he put down his
pencil and looked up at his teacher. "The hurrieder I go,
the behinder I get," he sighed. So take *your* time. God
isn't rushing you.

3. Don't sound like a broken record. God is not
absentminded, and he *did* hear you the first time. You
don't have to remind him of what you just said.

4. Ask for guidance. All of us lose our sense of direction
from time to time. Some of us even get lost. A nurse
overheard two elderly ladies in a hospital ward. "Where
do I go now?" asked one.

"Where do you want to go?" queried the other.

The first lady sighed in exasperation. "How do I know
where I want to go if I don't know where I am?"

God not only knows where you are, but where you
ought to be heading. Ask for guidance. If you listen, he'll
show you the way.

5. Don't hold back. I once talked to a young man
named John Tibbins. He absolutely refused to go for
counseling, though he admitted that he probably should.
"There are some things about me that I don't want
anyone else to know!" he protested. We're all a little like
that. What John meant was that he didn't want to tell
another human being everything about himself. It was
one thing to learn to live with his own shortcomings and
quite another to have the whole world in on the act. John

couldn't take the chance of having to watch himself shrink under critical eyes. But God's eyes aren't critical. Do as the old hymn tells you and "take it to the Lord in prayer."

6. Give God a chance. Leave a few spaces of silence. We're talking about conversation, which is a two-way street. You don't have to keep up a constant, one-sided babble. Give yourself a break. Take time to listen. Try speaking in short sentences. You can often say quite a lot in just a word or two. I've seen pretty dramatic results with just one word: "Fire!" You don't have to be that dramatic, but you *can* try to keep it simple.

7. Save your bargaining for the second-hand shop. Remember that God is not a used-car dealer. If you feel like making promises, wonderful. But try not to make promises that are impossible to keep, and refrain from asking for the world on a platter.

8. Be spontaneous. Everything in life doesn't have to be scheduled. Say what you think and feel at that very moment. Turn to God intuitively and speak to him freely.

9. Look around, and say, "Thank you!" There's plenty that you should be grateful for.

10. Say you're happy; say you're glad; say you're sorry; say anything you want to say . . . but say it out loud. Make the effort. Resist the temptation to close your eyes and take the easy way out. The oldest excuse in the book is "I know what I want to say, but I just can't put it into words." You *can't*. . . or you're too lazy to try? If you tried a trick like that in a classroom, you'd flunk the course. Listen, you can also be a failure at prayer. So make a stab at organizing your feelings into coherent form. Use your voice to verbalize your thoughts. There's nothing quite as effective as words for saying what you mean.

Take advantage of the miracle month of December to find something brand new in the performance of prayer. The curtain is going up, and *your* seat is in the front row. This time you're going to be more than a bystander. Every single morning, take time out to take a coffee break with God. Greet him with an open heart. Talk to him. Communicate. It's the surest way I know to find **an** important part of you that's been missing.

> *Guide me, Father*
> *As I open my eyes.*
> *Teach me,*
> *As I speak aloud.*
> *Lift the curtains of life*
> *And show me new horizons*
> *As I listen for the sound*
> *Of your voice.*

AFTERTHOUGHT

It's December thirty-first. How do you feel about yourself today? Have you stretched a little taller toward that vision of yourself as a whole person? You've had twelve whole months to practice. Was it enough? Maybe you expected to emerge at the end of a year with a shining halo and shimmering wings and not another problem to face for the rest of your life. Not likely!

I do believe in miracles, but the miracle of life is not an arrival at a whistle-stop. It's found in the steady growth and change that makes the whole trip worthwhile. If you have taken one step forward, even a stumbling one, you've put a missing piece of the jigsaw back into place. If you've stretched out your hand this year to another human being, you've made progress. If you have half an ounce of self-respect that you lacked before, if you straightened one closet, or shook your head with conviction, or laughed aloud, you're pointed in the right direction.

Here it is in a nutshell: God's vision for you and me doesn't come about in leaps and bounds. It's a slow process. Sometimes painful, sometimes joyous, but always worthwhile. Every single effort you make, no matter how small it might seem, is another building block cemented into the pattern of your life.

If you still feel that you have a long way to go . . . if you're afraid that a large piece of you is still missing . . . cheer up! None of us have finished the race yet. You do the very best you can with every single day, and *you're not out of time.* Tomorrow is just around the corner. It's called January first. You'll read all about it back at the beginning of this book. It's the day that signals a new beginning. It's a fresh start. Is that what you're looking for? I am. Let's turn back the pages . . . and begin all over again.